Brief Biographies

# Famous
# Composers

Theodore Rowland-Entwistle

and

Jean Cooke

## DAVID & CHARLES

NEWTON ABBOT  LONDON  VANCOUVER

ISBN 0 7153 6375 1

Set in 11 on 13pt Baskerville
and printed in Great Britain
by W J Holman Limited Dawlish
for David & Charles (Holdings) Limited
South Devon House Newton Abbot Devon

Published in Canada
by Douglas David & Charles Limited
3645 McKechnie Drive West Vancouver BC

# FOREWORD

Out of the many hundreds of people who have composed music it is difficult to choose 180 or so to form a representative selection. We have tried to include in this volume not only the obvious great names, but also composers whose music is frequently played. We have also selected names important in the history of western music from the thirteenth century to the present day. Some composers are included particularly because of their influence on the work of others, or as leaders of a country's musical development.

The 'main compositions' are by no means complete lists of a composer's works, but aim to give an idea of the scope of his work, plus the names of the most popular or well-known. Where dates are given for compositions these are generally those of first performance. Dates for writing are often difficult to establish, and the work may have gone on over many years. However, as far as possible works are listed in order of composition, which is why some dates may appear out of sequence. A name printed in small capitals in a biography indicates that the person so marked has his own entry.

All dates are given by the Gregorian calendar now in use. This calendar was introduced by Pope Gregory XIII in 1582 to correct the Julian calendar that preceded it, which had become ten days out of step with the seasons. Some countries did not adopt this reformed calendar until much later— Britain, for example, in 1752, and Russia in 1918, which explains why the Russian 'October Revolution' actually took place in November.

Place names are, as far as possible, given in both their contemporary forms and their present-day forms.

Academies and schools for the teaching of music go under many different names. We have used the general term 'conservatory' for all of them, except where a specific name is given.

Finally, we would like to acknowledge the help given to us by Mrs Pamela Haines and the rest of the staff of Hastings Reference Library, and the skill and determination shown by Mrs Kay Elder and Miss Jane Cressy in deciphering our often difficult manuscript.

T. R-E.
J. C.

ADAM DE LA HALLE (*c.* 1240–*c.* 1306) was a French *trouvère* or minstrel, born probably in Arras which was the capital of the French province of Artois. He was also known as 'Adam Le Bossu' or 'Le Bossu d'Arras' (*bossu* means hunchbacked). The trouvères were poet-musicians of northern France who wrote courtly love poems intended to be sung rather than recited. Like his fellow trouvères of Arras, Adam carried on this tradition, but he was the first to write simple songs in parts, and so point the way to the later style of polyphonic writing known as 'Ars Nova'. Many of his songs, motets and rondeaux still survive. His best work is *Le Jeu de Robin et Marion*, which tells the story of a knight who courts a shepherdess. It is a mixture of verse and songs, which were sung, probably unaccompanied, to tunes already popular. Adam spent some time at the court of the King of Naples.

MAIN COMPOSITIONS dramas: *Le Jeu Adam* (*c.* 1262), *Le Jeu de Robin et Marion* (*c.* 1275); chansons; rondeaux; motets.

ALBÉNIZ, ISAAC (1860–1909) was a Spanish pianist whose use of native rhythms and melodic turns of phrase made him one of the outstanding exponents of the Spanish nationalist school. He gave his first piano performance in Barcelona at the age of four. When he was seven he was refused permission to study at the Paris conservatory because he was too young, and so he was sent instead to Madrid. At nine years old he ran away and demonstrated an unusual degree of independence by giving concerts in different parts of Spain and then hiding away on a boat to cross the Atlantic. He supported himself by giving recitals all over the United States and Cuba before going to England at thirteen. He then spent a year studying at Leipzig and finally returned to Spain with no money. A royal grant made it possible for him to study in Brussels, and later he was able to go to Budapest for further tuition from FRANZ LISZT.

Albéniz also showed talent as a conductor. For a time he conducted *zarzuelas*, the traditional Spanish comic operettas which consist of songs and choruses interspersed with spoken dialogue. When he was about thirty he began to devote more time to composition, and while in Paris his style was influenced by CLAUDE DEBUSSY, PAUL DUKAS, and VINCENT D'INDY. His piano music is brilliant and technically difficult to play.

MAIN COMPOSITIONS operas: *The Magic Opal* (1893), *San Antonio de la Florida* (1894), *Enrico Clifford* (1895), *Pepita Jiménez* (1896); *Iberia* and many other piano works; orchestral pieces.

ARCADELT, JACOB (*c.* 1505–*c.* 1567), born in Flanders (now part of Belgium), spent most of his working life in Italy. He was one of a number of Netherlands musicians imported into Italy about that time, and was one of the first composers of the true Italian madrigal. He appears to have gone to Italy about 1538, and was in the service of the Pope the following year as a singer in the Sistine Chapel. He was later *maestro di cappella*. While he lived in Italy he took a year's leave of absence during which he visited France, and in the early 1550s he left the Pope's service for good.

In 1555 Arcadelt was in the employ of the Cardinal Duke of Guise, and went with him to Paris. Two years later he was a member of the French king's Chapel Royal, where he appears to have spent the rest of his life. An *Ave Maria* said to be his is a nineteenth-century arrangement of a three-part song by him.

MAIN COMPOSITIONS more than 200 Italian madrigals; 20 motets; 3 books of Masses; other Church music; many songs.

ARNE, THOMAS AUGUSTINE (1710–78), an English composer, wrote 'Rule, Britannia', and many still-popular settings of Shakespeare's songs. His father, an upholsterer, intended him to be a lawyer, but Arne was so devoted to music that he was allowed to follow his chosen career. He became an accomplished violinist. As a young man he often visited the opera disguised as a footman in order to get in free, and he began writing music for his sister, Susanna (later famous as the actress Mrs Cibber).

Arne's work attracted the attention of theatre managers, and by the time he was thirty he was busy writing operas, masques, and incidental music to plays. For some time he was official composer and band leader at Drury Lane Theatre, and from 1745 was also composer for Vauxhall Gardens, a fashionable London pleasure ground. His style is natural but elegant, and despite Italian influences typically English.

MAIN COMPOSITIONS oratorios: *The Death of Abel* (1744), *Judith* (1761); 52 operas and other stage works including *Rosamund* (1733), *Dido and Aeneas* (1734), *Alfred* (including 'Rule, Britannia', 1740), *Thomas and Sally* (1760); songs; organ concertos; harpsichord sonatas; chamber music.

ARNOLD, MALCOLM (born 1921), made a name as one of the most carefree as well as one of the more prolific of English composers in the twentieth century. He began his musical career as principal trumpet with the London Philharmonic Orchestra in 1941, serving in the army for a while during World War II. He first made his name as a composer with the overture *Beckus the Dandipratt* (a dandiprat is an urchin). In 1948 he won a scholarship that enabled him to study in Italy, after which he made his living as a composer and conductor.

Arnold's music is distinguished by its persistent sense of fun, and freedom from any sense of self-importance. Its easy approach has made it instantly popular with audiences and has procured it a ready hearing.

MAIN COMPOSITIONS operas; orchestral: six symphonies, concertos, overtures *Beckus the Dandipratt, Tam o' Shanter, Peterloo;* chamber music; vocal works.

BACH, CARL PHILIPP EMANUEL (1714–88), the second surviving son of JOHANN SEBASTIAN BACH and his first wife Maria Barbara, was the most successful of Johann Sebastian's children. He absorbed from his father (his principal teacher)

9

the technique and character of Baroque music, but succeeded in breaking new ground. Bach studied music with his father, and then law at Frankfurt University. When Bach was twenty-six Frederick the Great of Prussia, a keen musician and flautist, appointed him to be the king's official accompanist at Potsdam. There he stayed for twenty-seven years, finding his duties restricting and rather boring. Eventually Frederick allowed him to go to Hamburg as *Kapellmeister* in succession to his godfather, GEORG PHILIPP TELEMANN. In Hamburg Bach controlled the music of five churches, and lived in some comfort. He had an international reputation as a composer and as a player on the harpsichord and clavichord. He was a pioneer of what is known as sonata or first-movement form.

Bach's music and his writings had great influence on the work of JOSEPH HAYDN, WOLFGANG MOZART, and LUDWIG VAN BEETHOVEN. Mozart once said of him 'He is the parent, we are the children.' His *Essay on the True Art of Playing Keyboard Instruments* (published 1753-62) is one of the best guides to the style of playing of his day, and laid the foundation of modern pianoforte technique.

MAIN COMPOSITIONS oratorios: *The Israelites in the Desert, The Resurrection and Ascension of Jesus*; Church music including a Magnificat, 22 Passions, cantatas; orchestral: 18 symphonies, 52 piano concertos; 210 keyboard pieces; trio sonatas; 250 songs.

BACH, JOHANN CHRISTIAN (1735–82), the youngest son of JOHANN SEBASTIAN BACH and his second wife Anna Magdalena, is known as the 'English Bach' because he spent the last twenty years of his life in London. He wrote a considerable amount of charming and elegant music in the so-called 'galant' style, and he had a great influence on the young WOLFGANG AMADEUS MOZART, who studied with Bach during his stay in London.

Bach was just fifteen when his father died. He went to live and to study with his step-brother, CARL PHILIPP EMANUEL

BACH, in Berlin. Later he went to Italy and was appointed organist at Milan Cathedral, but neglected his duties in order to write operas. These operas brought him fame and an invitation to become composer to the King's Theatre in London. There he spent a crowded life writing, teaching the new pianoforte, and organising an annual season of concerts. Worn out with overwork, he died at the age of forty-six.

MAIN COMPOSITIONS operas: *Artaserse* (1761), *Catone* (1761), *Alessandro nell'Indie* (1762), *Orione* (1763), *Zanida* (1763), *Adriano in Siria* (1765), *Carattaco* (1766), *La Clemenza de Scipione* (1778); other works for the theatre; Church music; songs; piano works.

BACH, JOHANN SEBASTIAN (1685–1750), was the greatest member of a family of almost forty musicians, whose working lives spanned more than 200 years. Bach was the son of a violinist at Eisenach, a small town now in Thuringia, East Germany, near the border with West Germany. Both his parents died while he was young, and Bach was brought up by his elder brother, Johann Christoph. When he was fifteen Bach became a choirboy at Lüneburg, 64km (40 miles) south-east of Hamburg. Three years later he was back in Thuringia, first as a violinist at Weimar, and then as organist at Arnstadt.

Two years later Bach took some leave and walked more than 320km (200 miles) to Lübeck in the very north of Germany to hear DIETRICH BUXTEHUDE, famous as one of the greatest organists of his day. It seems likely that he also hoped to secure the succession to Buxtehude's post as organist of St Mary's, Lübeck, but apparently did not like the condition that he would have to marry one of Buxtehude's five daughters. Bach overstayed his leave, and in other respects the authorities at Arnstadt were not best pleased with him, so it is hardly surprising that a year later he moved to another post at Mühlhausen, also in Thuringia, marrying at the same time his cousin Maria Barbara Bach. But an inadequate salary and religious differences led Bach to look very quickly for another post, and within a year he was in Weimar, as court organist and violinist to Duke Wilhelm Ernst. There, though as a servant (the rank accorded to court musicians, however talented) he had to wear livery, he spent several happy and productive years. But when he was passed over for promotion to the post of *Kapellmeister* (musical director), he obtained the post of *Kapellmeister* at Köthen.

Bach spent six years at Köthen, and these gave him a break from the duties of an organist, and turned his attention towards orchestral and chamber music. There he wrote his keyboard suites, the music for violin and cello, and the set of six concertos he dedicated to the Margrave of Brandenburg. He also wrote the first book of his preludes and fugues for keyboard. During this time his wife died, leaving him with four young children (three others died in infancy). About eighteen months later he married again—a twenty-year-old soprano, Anna Magdalena Wilcken. For her he wrote a set of pieces to teach her the harpsichord, now known as *Anna Magdalena's Clavier Book.*

In order to find schools for his elder sons, Bach decided to move to the large city of Leipzig (Weimar had only about 5,000 people), and at the age of thirty-eight he became cantor at St Thomas's Church there. It was a step down from being *Kapellmeister.* His duties involved training and conducting choirs and an orchestra, and trying to please the Leipzig town council as well as the authorities at St Thomas's. There were many difficulties, but Bach held this post for the rest of his life. Part of his work consisted of providing a continual supply of fresh music for the church, and he produced an average of a cantata a month for more than twenty years. Gradually his fame spread, and he had many admirers in high places. When he was sixty-two he went by invitation to visit Frederick the Great, the Prussian ruler, at Potsdam, where his son CARL PHILIPP EMANUEL BACH was accompanist. When he arrived the king exclaimed delightedly 'Gentlemen, old Bach is come!' and insisted he should sit down at once to play. Like his great contemporary GEORGE FRIDERIC

HANDEL, Bach lost his sight in his last years. He died with his last composition, *The Art of Fugue*, unfinished. His music was forgotten for nearly a hundred years until FELIX MENDELSSOHN revived it.

Of his many children, most died in infancy, as was common in those days. The eldest son, Wilhelm Friedmann, had great talent but an unfortunate disposition which prevented him from achieving much, but three other sons, Carl Philipp Emanuel, Johann Christoph, and JOHANN CHRISTIAN, all made their mark as musicians.

MAIN COMPOSITIONS orchestral: 6 Brandenburg concertos, 4 suites, concertos for violin, harpsichord, flute; Church music: *Magnificat* (1723), *Passion According to St John* (1723), *Passion According to St Matthew* (1729), *Christmas Oratorio* (1734), *Easter Oratorio* (1736), *B Minor Mass* (1738), 250 cantatas; 23 secular cantatas; organ preludes, toccatas and other works; clavier (harpsichord or clavichord): *48 Preludes and Fugues* (*The Well-Tempered Clavier*), *Goldberg Variations*, English suites, French suites, Italian concerto; chamber music: violin, cello, and flute sonatas, trios, *The Musical Offering* (1749), *The Art of Fugue* (1750).

BALAKIREV, MILI ALEKSEEVICH (1837–1910), a Russian pianist, was a leader of the nationalist movement in Russian music. He collected Russian folk tunes and used them as themes for his own compositions. As a boy he had access to a private orchestra kept by a rich family friend, and he became a conductor and also a gifted pianist. He was greatly influenced by MIKHAIL GLINKA, and he founded a group of musicians known as 'The Five' (the other members were C. A. Cui, ALEKSANDR BORODIN, MODESTE MUSSORGSKY, and NIKOLAI RIMSKY-KORSAKOV). They were all strongly nationalist in outlook, and also amateur musicians. Balakirev also founded and directed the Free School of Music in St Petersburg (now Leningrad), devoted to Russian music. Between 1871 and 1876 Balakirev had some kind of breakdown, during which he gave up music and became a railway clerk. But he recovered, returned to music and pursued an active career as conductor, teacher, and composer until he retired about 1900.

MAIN COMPOSITIONS orchestral: 2 symphonies, overtures, symphonic poem *Tamara* (1867); music for *King Lear;* choral works; chamber music; piano music including 2 concertos; songs.

BARBER, SAMUEL (born 1910), an American, combined traditional treatment of form, melody and harmony with a freshness of approach. He began playing the piano as a boy, and later added singing and composition to his studies. At the age of twenty-five he was awarded the *Prix de Rome* (which entitles the winner to study at the Academy of Rome). Later he became the first musician to win two Pulitzer Prizes. Barber's compositions range over a wide field—songs, operas, orchestral works, concertos, and chamber music. His *Adagio* for strings (arranged from the slow movement of a string quartet) won wide popularity both in Europe and in the United States. Barber himself recorded the vocal part of *Dover Beach,* a setting for voice and string quartet of a poem by Matthew Arnold.

MAIN COMPOSITIONS operas: *Vanessa* (1958 Pulitzer Prize), *Antony and Cleopatra* (1966); ballet *Medea* (1946); symphonies; concertos for violin, cello, piano (1963 Pulitzer Prize); vocal: *Dover Beach* (1931), *Knoxville, Summer of 1915* (1947); chamber music; songs.

BARTÓK, BÉLA (1881–1945), a Hungarian pianist and collector of folk tunes, played an important part in the development of music in the early part of the twentieth century. He showed considerable skill in music as a child, and at the age of eighteen entered the Hungarian Royal Academy of Music, Budapest, where he studied composition and the piano. He was at first greatly influenced by the music of JOHANNES BRAHMS and by ERNÖ DOHNÁNYI; later he fell under

14

the spell of FRANZ LISZT, RICHARD WAGNER, and RICHARD STRAUSS.

But the real influence in Bartók's life was the folk music of the Magyars, the Slovaks, and the Romanians. He discovered old scales—the modes—still in use, and this led him to forsake the ordinary major and minor scales and treat all twelve notes of the scale as equal. Bartók's lifelong friend, ZOLTÁN KODÁLY, joined him in his work of collecting folk tunes. At the age of twenty-six Bartók became a professor of the piano at the Budapest academy; but his compositions did not at first find favour with public or critics. His first real success came in 1917 when his ballet *The Wooden Prince* was performed in Budapest.

During the 1920s Bartók's music became increasingly popular. But political events in Europe made Hungary a place where he could no longer be happy, and he emigrated to the United States in 1940. His last years were spent in poverty, his health was deteriorating rapidly, and after a spell in hospital he died.

Among Bartók's works his six string quartets are regarded as the most significant, while piano students find his *Mikrokosmos,* a collection of 153 piano pieces of graded difficulty, an invaluable aid to mastering the techniques and ideas of twentieth-century music. His experimental work and innovations have been of great influence on later composers. In addition to his own work, he collected, edited and published over 6,000 folk tunes, from Hungary, Romania, and Arab countries.

MAIN COMPOSITIONS opera *Duke Bluebeard's Castle* (1911); ballets: *The Wooden Prince* (1917), *The Miraculous Mandarin* (1926); orchestral: suites, music for strings, percussion and celesta (1936), 3 piano concertos, concerto for orchestra; chamber music including 6 string quartets; piano music; choral works; songs.

BAX, SIR ARNOLD EDWARD TREVOR (1883–1953), was an English composer who came under the influence of

Celtic lore and literature—though he had no known Celtic ancestors. He was a master of the technical side of composition and orchestration, but used his great abilities to express feeling rather than for their own sake. Even as a boy he could read complicated musical scores easily, and this facility led him to produce an early string quartet that was almost too difficult to perform. In his later works Bax deliberately simplified his writing, relying on variation in harmony, melody and orchestration to give richness to his music.

Bax spent many years of his life in Ireland or Scotland. He wrote short stories and poems under the pen-name Dermot O'Byrne, all strongly influenced by Celtic tradition. He wrote a good deal of chamber music, while his piano music included a concertante for left hand alone for the pianist Harriet Cohen, who injured her right hand in an accident. In 1937 he was knighted, and five years later he was appointed Master of the King's Musick.

MAIN COMPOSITIONS ballet: *The Truth about the Russian Dancers* (1920); orchestral: 7 symphonies, tone poems *In the Faëry Hills* (1909), *The Garden of Fand* (1916), *Tintagel* (1917), *November Woods* (1917), *The Tale the Pine Tree Knew* (1931), concertos for violin, viola, cello, piano, *Overture to a Picaresque Comedy* (1930); choral music: *Mater Ora Filium* (1921), *St Patrick's Breastplate* (1924), *The Morning Watch* (1935); chamber music including sonata for viola and harp; works for one and two pianos; songs; film music.

BEETHOVEN, LUDWIG VAN (1770–1827), a German pianist, was one of the greatest composers who ever lived. His work marks the end of the so-called 'Classical' music of the eighteenth century and the beginning of the 'Romantic' movement of the nineteenth. His bold, rugged, and dramatic style makes a complete break with the sophisticated elegance of his immediate predecessors, WOLFGANG AMADEUS MOZART and JOSEPH HAYDN. By his stormy, independent attitude he helped to free musicians from the position of servants which they had hitherto held.

Beethoven was born in Bonn, of Flemish ancestry, the son of a chorister in the service of the Archbishop-Elector of Cologne. Drunkenness prevented Beethoven's father from rising higher in his profession. Beethoven studied music from an early age, and became deputy court organist at the age of fourteen. Three years later he went to Vienna and studied for a few months with Mozart, but had to return to help look after his family. It was not until he was twenty-two that he was able to leave Bonn and settle in Vienna, where there was much more scope for promising musicians. He had lessons from several leading musicians, including Haydn, and quickly acquired a reputation as a pianist. During this time he was befriended by several wealthy patrons. With their aid, a number of successful public concerts, and the publication of some of his music, he began to prosper.

When he was twenty-nine Beethoven suffered the first blow in a tragedy that was to change the whole course of his life: he began to go deaf. For a while this did not prevent him from continuing his career as a brilliant pianist, but despite treatment his hearing grew gradually worse. Saddened but undaunted, he worked even harder at composing, perhaps realising subconsciously that composition might soon be the only form of music making left to him. His life became more and more lonely. He was a naturally suspicious and quarrelsome man, and his deafness made both these traits worse. Fortunately, when he was thirty-eight, three of his wealthy patrons banded together to provide him with a pension for life, and though—this was at the height of the Napoleonic Wars—the value of money dropped sharply, he always had at least enough to support him.

By 1815 Beethoven was so deaf that he was no longer able to play in public, and he was having trouble in conducting. Seven years later his attempts to conduct a rehearsal for a revival of his only opera, *Fidelio*, ended in disaster, and when he was fifty-four he was totally unable to hear the storm of applause that greeted the first performance of his ninth symphony. His last years were saddened not only by deafness but by a series of lawsuits over the custody of his nephew, Karl, a worthless and selfish youth, and by illness.

Beethoven's greatest contribution to music was his development of the symphony. His nine symphonies were on a much larger and grander scale than those of his predecessors. Hardly less important was his development of the piano sonata. His 32 sonatas are often called the pianist's 'New Testament', the 48 Preludes and Fugues of JOHANN SEBASTIAN BACH forming the 'Old Testament'. His music made demands on the piano that led quickly to its development as we know it today. And in the string quartets he wrote in his last years he reached emotional heights that make enormous demands on the musicianship of the players.

MAIN COMPOSITIONS opera: *Fidelio* (1805); orchestral: 9 symphonies, 6 overtures, 5 piano concertos, 1 violin concerto, triple concerto for piano, violin and cello; incidental music; chamber music: 17 string quartets, 10 violin and piano sonatas, quintet, sextets, septet, and octet; piano solos: 32 sonatas, bagatelles, rondos; songs.

BELLINI, VINCENZO (1801–35), an Italian opera composer, was noted for his flowing melodies, which gave singers every chance to display their voices and their technique. He was born in Sicily, the son of an organist, and his early talent led a Sicilian nobleman to pay for his lessons in Naples. While still a student Bellini was commissioned to write an opera, *Adelson e Salvina*, for the Naples opera house. Its success led to a commission for La Scala, Milan, and his fame was assured. His most famous works were *La Sonnambula* and *Norma*, but his later operas suffered from poor librettos. He had bad health all his life, and died during a visit to Paris just before his 34th birthday.

MAIN COMPOSITIONS *Adelson e Salvina* (1825), *Bianca e Fernando* (1826), *Il Pirata* (1827), *I Capuletti ed i Montecchi* (1830), *La Sonnambula* (1831), *Norma* (1831), *Beatrice di Tenda* (1833), *I Puritani* (1835).

BERG, ALBAN (1885–1935), an Austrian, was a pupil and friend of ARNOLD SCHÖNBERG, whose 'note-row' method of composition he adopted. He spent most of his life quietly in Vienna, his birthplace, teaching composition for a living. He suffered greatly from asthma. He is best known for his opera *Wozzeck*, completed in 1921 before he adopted the twelve-note technique of his master. It caused a sensation at its first performance in Berlin in 1925—after 137 rehearsals. It is divided into a large number of short scenes, each in some musical form such as fugue or sonata. Berg's second opera, *Lulu*, was unfinished when he died. He also wrote some chamber and orchestral music.

MAIN COMPOSITIONS operas: *Wozzeck* (1925), *Lulu* (1937); chamber music; chamber concerto for piano, violin, and wind (1925); violin concerto (1935); *Der Wein* (for soprano and orchestra, 1920); songs.

BERIO, LUCIANO (born 1923), an Italian conductor and music director, spent a number of years experimenting with electronic music. In his compositions for normal instruments and voices he was greatly influenced by the serial music of PIERRE BOULEZ, whom he admired greatly. Berio began his career as an opera house coach and conductor, which fostered his love of opera. In 1952 he went to the United States, where he first encountered electronic music. He also studied there with LUIGI DALLAPICCOLA, who introduced him to the serial method of composition. He returned to Italy and joined the staff of RAI, the Italian radio service. He went back to the United States some years later.

MAIN COMPOSITIONS operas: *Passagio* (1963), *Laborintus II* (1968); choral: *Tracce* (*Traces*); orchestral music; chamber music; songs; electronic music.

BERKELEY, LENNOX RANDAL FRANCIS (born 1903), a British composer partly of French descent, studied in Paris under NADIA BOULANGER; this developed the French side of his nature rather than the English. His work tends to have a crisp self-restraint about it, though many of his compositions are warmly lyrical. Though his output includes many fine chamber works, it is in his writing for orchestra that his talents are best displayed. After several years on the music staff of the BBC he became professor of composition at the Royal Academy of Music, London, and spent much of his life teaching.

MAIN COMPOSITIONS operas: *Nelson* (1953), *A Dinner Engagement* (1954), *Ruth* (1956); orchestral: symphonies, *Divertimento*, *Serenade*, concertos for piano, flute, violin, suite *Winter's Tale*, partita for chamber orchestra; works for voice and orchestra; chamber music; piano solos; film music.

BERLIOZ, (LOUIS) HECTOR (1803–69), a leading French Romantic composer, was a master of orchestration, and also loved gigantic forces. Ideally, he would have preferred an orchestra of three hundred players or more. But he could and did emphasise subtle, clear contrasts of tone colour. Almost all his music was written to a 'programme'—it told a story of some kind.

His father set him to study medicine, but Berlioz rebelled in favour of music, paying for his own studies by singing in an opera chorus. He had several violent love affairs, eventually marrying the Irish actress Harriet Smithson. After some years they separated, and he lived with Marie Recio, a singer, whom he married when his first wife died. He made his living largely by writing musical criticism and by conducting.

In 1832, the violin virtuoso, NICCOLÓ PAGANINI, commissioned a viola concerto from him. As Berlioz wrote it, the work was a symphony for orchestra with viola obbligato, *Harold in Italy*. Paganini would not play it, but when he heard it performed he knelt in homage before Berlioz, and next day sent him a cheque for 20,000 francs. This freed the composer from drudgery for a time.

To succeed in France in Berlioz's time a composer had to write operas. The intrigues of his enemies ensured that

Berlioz's first opera, *Benvenuto Cellini*, was a failure, and for this reason he never enjoyed quite the fame that should have been his. But his influence was felt all over Europe, which he toured many times as a conductor.

MAIN COMPOSITIONS operas: *Benvenuto Cellini* (1838), *Beatrice and Benedict* (1862), *The Trojans* (1859); symphonies: *Fantastic Symphony* (1830), *Harold in Italy* (1834), *Romeo and Juliet* (1839); choral works, including *Te Deum* (1849), *Requiem* (1837); oratorio *The Childhood of Christ* (1854); songs; overture. THEORETICAL WORKS several books on music.

BIZET, GEORGES (1838–75), a French opera composer, is remembered mainly for two popular works—the Spanish gipsy opera *Carmen* and the incidental music to Alphonse Daudet's play *L'Arlésienne* (*The Girl from Arles*). Bizet, son of a hairdresser, showed great musical gifts from boyhood. He had a busy life as a teacher, while writing a succession of operas. They brought him little credit, and his despair is shown by the large number of other operas he began and did not finish. During the Franco-Prussian War of 1870–1 Bizet served in the army, and his finest work was composed after this break. *Carmen*, his last work, was not well received in Paris, and Bizet died just three months after its first performance, before it became a world-wide success. He was a brilliant pianist, but preferred not to be a soloist.

MAIN COMPOSITIONS operas: *The Pearl Fishers* (1863), *The Fair Maid of Perth* (1867), *Djamileh* (1872), *Carmen* (1875); orchestral: suite from *L'Arlésienne*, symphony *Rome*, suite *Children's Games* (originally piano duet); choral works; piano solos; songs.

BLISS, SIR ARTHUR (born 1891), brought a mixture of Romanticism and Classicism to English music of the twentieth century, combined with a willingness to experiment that prevented any suggestion of old-fashionedness. As a young man he served in the army during World War I, and

21

was wounded. His experiences revolted him for a time against pure Romanticism, but his vivid imagination and desire to experiment led him to produce such novel works as his *Colour Symphony*, in which each movement is inspired by a different colour, and to use voices instrumentally.

Bliss's ballet music is among the most popular of his many works. The first was *Checkmate*, produced in Paris in 1937. The second was *Miracle in the Gorbals*, whose music matched its sensationally tragic story. From both these, as from some of his film music, Bliss made orchestral suites.

After a spell as professor at the University of California, Bliss served for a time as director of music of the British Broadcasting Corporation. His work brought him a knighthood, and later his appointment as Master of the Queen's Musick.

MAIN COMPOSITIONS operas: *The Olympians* (1948), *Tobias and the Angel* (TV 1960); ballets: *Checkmate* (1937), *Miracle in the Gorbals* (1944), *Adam Zero* (1946), *The Lady of Shalott* (1958); orchestral: *A Colour Symphony* (1922), concertos for orchestra, piano, violin, suites, studies; voices and instruments: *Madam Noy* (1918), *Rhapsody* (1919), *Rout* (1920); chamber music; songs; film music.

BOCCHERINI, LUIGI (1743–1805), an Italian cellist, was a prolific writer of elegant chamber music. He studied in Rome, and then went on a brilliant concert tour. In 1769 he went to Madrid, where he became composer to the Spanish king's brother, the Infante Don Luis. Luis died in 1785, and Boccherini secured an appointment as court composer to King Friedrich Wilhelm II of Prussia. After the king's death he returned to Madrid.

MAIN COMPOSITIONS operas: *La Confederazione* (1765), *La Clementina* (1786); sacred works: Mass for four voices, *Christmas Cantata*, *Motets for Christmastime*; chamber music: 2 octets, 16 sextets, 155 quintets, 102 quartets, many trios and duos; orchestral: 20 symphonies, 1 suite, 4 cello concertos.

BORODIN, ALEKSANDR PORFIREVICH (1833–87), a Russian scientist, was one of the group known as 'The Five' founded by MILI BALAKIREV. He wrote only twenty-one works, composed in what little leisure he could snatch from his other work as professor of chemistry at the Medico-Surgical Academy at St Petersburg (Leningrad). His boyhood gift for music—he played the cello, flute, and piano—developed when he met Balakirev in his late twenties. His most famous work is the opera *Prince Igor,* completed after his death by his friends NIKOLAI RIMSKY-KORSAKOV and ALEKSANDR GLAZUNOV. The Polovtsian dances from the opera are often played as an orchestral piece. Borodin did important research on aldehydes, and also founded a school of medicine for women. He dropped dead at a ball when he was fifty-three.

MAIN COMPOSITIONS opera *Prince Igor* (1890); orchestral: 2 symphonies, symphonic sketch *In the Steppes of Central Asia*; chamber music; songs; piano music.

BOULANGER, NADIA JULIETTE (born 1887), a French teacher and conductor, had enormous influence on twentieth-century music through her pupils. She herself studied at the Paris conservatory under GABRIEL FAURÉ, and afterwards taught at the conservatory for a time. She had a number of early successes as a composer, but gave up composition when her more gifted sister Lili (1893–1918) died at the age of twenty-four. Lili wrote a number of works including two symphonic poems and some choral pieces.

Three years after her sister's death Nadia Boulanger became professor of the Conservatoire Américain, a music school for American students founded at Fontainebleu. Later she was its director. These posts led to many teaching and conducting visits to the United States. She also continued to teach at the Paris conservatory. She contributed greatly to musical learning through her interpretation and revival of old music, particularly that of CLAUDIO MONTEVERDI. Her main influence as a teacher was on American composers— AARON COPLAND, ROY HARRIS, WALTER PISTON, ROGER SES-

SIONS, and VIRGIL THOMSON were among her pupils. But she also taught a number of European composers including LENNOX BERKELEY and DARIUS MILHAUD.

MAIN COMPOSITIONS Cantata *Sirène* (1908); several short works.

BOULEZ, PIERRE (born 1925), a conductor, gained a worldwide reputation as the leading French composer of serial music, to the 'note-row' formula devised by ARNOLD SCHÖNBERG. He took the formula even further, applying the serial technique to rhythm, length of notes, and orchestration, producing a complex texture that has an apparent air of spontaneity.

Boulez studied at the Paris conservatory under OLIVIER MESSIAEN, who influenced him greatly and changed the course of his career (he had originally planned to be an engineer). For some years Boulez conducted an instrumental ensemble in Paris, giving concerts of contemporary music. In 1971 he became principal conductor of the BBC Symphony Orchestra in London, and also of the New York Philharmonic Orchestra.

MAIN COMPOSITIONS: *Polyphonie* X for 18 solo instruments (1951), *Visage Nuptial* (revised 1951), *Le Marteau sans Maître* (1954), *Deux Improvisations sur Mallarmé* (1957), *Soleil des Eaux* for chorus and orchestra (1958), *Pli selon Pli: Hommage à Mallarmé* (1960), *Éclat* (1964).

BOYCE, WILLIAM (c. 1710–79), an English organist and musical editor, is best known as a composer of Church music. He studied as a chorister at St Paul's Cathedral, London. In 1736 he was appointed composer to the Chapel Royal, and in 1765 became Master of the King's Musick. He was affected by deafness from an early age, and in 1769 he gave up all his posts except that of organist at the Chapel Royal. He spent most of the rest of his life teaching, and compiling a collection of English cathedral music. 'Heart of Oak' is the best known of his many songs.

MAIN COMPOSITIONS Church music: 63 anthems, 5 services; orchestral: 8 symphonies, 12 overtures; chamber music: 12 sonatas for two violins and bass (1747); stage music for 15 masques and plays; many songs, duets, and cantatas.

BRAHMS, JOHANNES (1833–97), a German pianist, continued the great symphonic tradition of LUDWIG VAN BEETHOVEN. During his lifetime there was much enmity between supporters of his music and that of RICHARD WAGNER, from which Brahms himself tried to hold aloof. Brahms was the son of a double-bass player, and early developed his skill as a pianist. By the time he was fourteen he was playing in dance halls and taverns to augment the family income. When he was twenty he teamed up with a Hungarian violinist, Eduard Reményi, with whom he embarked on a wandering tour of northern Germany, giving concerts where they could. Reményi introduced Brahms to Joseph Joachim, one of the leading violinists of the day, who recognised the young man's genius and introduced him to a number of influential people in the world of music. Among these people was FRANZ LISZT, for whom Brahms seems to have conceived an instant dislike.

Soon afterwards he was befriended by the composer and critic ROBERT SCHUMANN and his wife Clara. They treated him almost as a son and helped him to develop his talents; in return, when Schumann's mind gave way Brahms did his utmost to help Clara. For a time Brahms held an appointment at the little court of Detmold, while he also conducted a ladies' choir in Hamburg, his native city. But he failed in his application for the conductorship of the Hamburg Philharmonic concerts, and in disgust he decided to settle in Vienna, where he had already made some friends. There he settled down to a more or less regular life, conducting, playing, and composing. While he had many friends, he also made many enemies, because of his quick temper and acid tongue. Though he had a number of minor flirtations, he recoiled from the idea of marriage, perhaps realising that his irascibility would make him a bad husband. Even his friendship with Joachim ended in a quarrel.

Brahms's works are of a consistently high standard, and this is possibly because he destroyed a large part of all that he wrote. In his music Brahms combined the counterpoint of JOHANN SEBASTIAN BACH, which he much admired, with the symphonic style of Beethoven. It is full of complicated cross-rhythms, not easy to play but sounding entirely natural to the listener. To his mastery of melody we owe many fine songs and choral works.

MAIN COMPOSITIONS orchestral: 4 symphonies, 2 overtures, 2 piano concertos, violin concerto, double concerto for violin and cello; choral: *German Requiem* (1857), *Alto Rhapsody* (1869), *Song of Destiny* (1867); chamber music; piano solos; nearly 200 songs.

BRIAN, HAVERGAL (1876–1972), was one of the most neglected composers of the twentieth century. He is sometimes called 'the forgotten man of English music'. He established a local reputation for his orchestral and choral works in the early years of the century. But his great Gothic Symphony, written between 1919 and 1927, was rejected for performance, partly on the grounds that it needed enormous forces to play it. From then on Brian's work, large and small, was almost completely ignored.

Brian was not deterred. He continued to write a series of massive works, without making a serious attempt to persuade people to perform them. He was almost eighty before he heard any of his symphonies played, when three were performed out of the twelve he had then composed. He wrote twenty more before he died. His music is as massive in thought as it is in construction. He combines the majesty of the late Romantic movement with a constant quest for new ideas, and shows a mastery of form in all that he wrote. He lived long enough to know that his fellow musicians were at last beginning to recognise his greatness.

MAIN COMPOSITIONS 32 symphonies; 5 operas; choral works.

BRIDGE, FRANK (1879–1941), was an English musician whose modest and retiring nature helped to keep his music in comparative obscurity. He was a highly accomplished viola player, and it may well have been his love for the instrument that led him to devote so much of his energies to writing chamber music. He is probably better known for his songs, such as *Love Went A-Riding* and *O That It Were So.*

In his early works Bridge was a Romantic, but as time went on his music became more advanced in style, chromatic in harmony and eventually dissonant. But with it all he contrived to make his music straightforward to perform. Even in his orchestral music his command of instrumental technique prevented the works from being unnecessarily hard for the players. Bridge had a number of pupils, one of them being BENJAMIN BRITTEN, who was greatly influenced by him.

MAIN COMPOSITIONS orchestral: suite *The Sea* (1910), *Phantasm* for piano and orchestra; chamber music; piano solos; songs.


BRITTEN, (EDWARD) BENJAMIN (born 1913), a pianist and conductor, established himself as the leading British composer of the period after World War II. A precocious musician, he was writing music well before he was nine years old. When he was twenty-six he moved to the United States, where he spent three busy years composing. At this time he produced his first opera, *Paul Bunyan*, to a libretto by W. H. Auden. It was a failure. In 1942 Britten returned to England to help his war-torn country. A convinced pacifist, he would not fight, but contributed as much as he could to the war effort through music, playing in hospitals and air-raid shelters. During this time he wrote his second opera, *Peter Grimes*, which was an outstanding success.

Three years after the end of World War II Britten and his lifelong friend, the tenor Peter Pears, joined with the producer Eric Crozier in founding an annual music festival at Aldeburgh, the east-coast fishing village where Britten made his home. It has become an internationally important festival, where many first performances take place. Britten continued to write operas, and also much Church music, music, for children, and many fine song cycles. In his style he combined traditional aspects of music with the freedom of harmony and expression introduced by the more advanced musicians of the twentieth century.

MAIN COMPOSITIONS operas: *Peter Grimes* (1945), *The Rape of Lucretia* (1946), *Albert Herring* (1947), *Let's Make an Opera* (1949), *Billy Budd* (1951), *Gloriana* (1953), *Turn of the Screw* (1954), *A Midsummer Night's Dream* (1960), *Owen Wingrave* (TV, 1971), *Death in Venice* (1973); ballet: *The Prince of the Pagodas* (1957); Church dramas: *Noye's Fludde* (1957), *Curlew River* (1964), *The Burning Fiery Furnace* (1966), *The Prodigal Son* (1968); choral works including *A Boy Was Born*, *Saint Nicholas* (cantata), *A War Requiem*; orchestral music including *The Young Persons' Guide to the Orchestra* (variations on a theme of Purcell); works for piano, cello, violin and orchestra; organ and piano pieces; song cycles.

BRUCH, MAX (1838–1920), a German conductor, was famous in his own lifetime for his choral works, especially his epic-cantatas, but is now chiefly remembered for his beautiful violin concertos, especially the ever-popular concerto in G Minor. Bruch, whose mother was a distinguished singer, developed his musical talents early—he wrote his first symphony at fourteen. He won a scholarship which gave him four years' training under some leading teachers of the day. He spent most of his life as a conductor in Germany and England.

MAIN COMPOSITIONS operas; choral: *Frithjof* (1867), *Schön Ellen* (1867), *Odysseus* (1872), *Das Lied von der Glocke* (1878), *Das Feierkreuz* (1888); orchestral: 3 symphonies, 3 violin concertos; chamber music; songs.

BRUCKNER, (JOSEF) ANTON (1824–96), an Austrian organist and teacher, is widely appreciated in Germany and

Austria for his nine monumental symphonies, but his music is less widely played or appreciated elsewhere. The son of a village schoolmaster, he himself became one, after studying singing and the organ. In 1856 he was appointed organist of Linz Cathedral, and was able to travel frequently to Vienna to study composition. He became professor of the organ and composition at the Vienna conservatory, and later was also a lecturer at the city university.

Fame eluded Bruckner until his Symphony No 7 was performed in 1884. His music was strongly influenced by that of RICHARD WAGNER; it is large and inclined to be stolid. Its naturalness reflects the countryman that Bruckner always remained, even when he lived in the sophisticated city of Vienna. He was a devout Roman Catholic, and his work reflects his spiritual consciousness. His technique was never quite equal to the demands of his genius.

MAIN COMPOSITIONS 9 symphonies (the last incomplete), plus 2 early symphonies; 3 Masses, a *Te Deum*, and other sacred choral works; choruses for male voices; chamber music; songs.

BULL, JOHN (*c.* 1562–1628), an English organist and teacher, was a leading keyboard composer of his day. He studied as a choirboy in the Chapel Royal of Queen Elizabeth I. In 1582 he became organist of Hereford Cathedral, and three years later returned to the Chapel Royal, of which he became organist in 1591. Later the queen appointed him music professor at the newly founded Gresham College, London. He gave up the post in 1607 in order to marry. In 1613 Bull suddenly went to Brussels and entered the service of the Archduke Albert there; possibly he found his face no longer fitted at the court of James I. He is remembered for about 150 pieces for virginals and organ. One of these contains a melody which may be an ancestor of the British national anthem.

MAIN COMPOSITIONS 150 pieces for organ or virginals; some vocal music (mostly lost); 50 pieces for viols.

BUXTEHUDE, DIETRICH (c. 1637–1707), a Danish organist, was one of the greatest players of his time. The son of an organist, he held his first appointments in Denmark. In 1668 he was appointed organist of St Mary's, Lübeck, in northern Germany, marrying, as a condition of his employment, the daughter of his predecessor. There he remained until his death, his great skill as composer and player for the instrument drawing other musicians to Lübeck to hear him. Among them were GEORGE FRIDERIC HANDEL and JOHANN SEBASTIAN BACH, both of whom hoped to succeed him; but neither would agree to the condition that they must marry one of Buxtehude's five daughters. Buxtehude's vocal and instrumental music is simple in construction, though some of it is attractively decorated. Bach undoubtedly owed much to his study of Buxtehude's work.

MAIN COMPOSITIONS organ toccatas, preludes, fugues, and other pieces; suites for harpsichord (mostly lost); string sonatas; Church cantatas.

BYRD, WILLIAM (c. 1543–1623) was an Englishman whose wide range of music made him the most important composer of the Elizabethan age. He was senior chorister at St Paul's Cathedral, studied with THOMAS TALLIS and became organist of Lincoln Cathedral. Although Byrd was a Roman Catholic he wrote much Church music to English words as well as to Latin texts, and managed to remain faithful to Rome while being a loyal member of Queen Elizabeth's Protestant Chapel Royal. Apart from his church music, Byrd wrote much music for the organ and virginals, and his fantasias for viol consort led the way for later composers. With Tallis he was granted a monopoly in music printing for a number of years, and together the composers produced books of sacred and secular choral music, instrumental works, and keyboard pieces which found their way into the *Fitzwilliam Virginal Book*.

In 1588 the first volume of a collection of Italian madrigals known as *Musica Transalpina* (*Music from across the Alps*) was introduced into England by Nicholas Yonge, but although

Byrd contributed to the publication and was influenced by the Italian style, he still clung to the older form of writing for solo voice with instrumental accompaniment.

MAIN COMPOSITIONS *Cantiones Sacrae* (1575, 1589, 1591), *Psalmes, Sonets, and Songs of Sadnes and Pietie* (1588), *Gradualia* (1605, 1607); Masses; anthems; music for virginals.

CAGE, JOHN MILTON (born 1912), an American pianist and teacher, produced some of the most revolutionary music of the twentieth century. His natural interest in experiment and innovation was stimulated by his teachers, who included ARNOLD SCHÖNBERG and EDGARD VARÈSE. In addition to the twelve-tone techniques of Schönberg, Cage was attracted to ANTON WEBERN's use of periods of silence. From this he graduated to the use of percussion, and to drawing unusual sounds from the ordinary piano. To this end he invented the 'prepared piano', stuffing all manner of materials in and around the strings before the performance so that the instrument emitted clunks, thuds, and other abnormal noises.

By the time he was forty Cage was experimenting with any kind of noise-maker as a source of music. He was a pioneer of 'concrete music', in which manipulation of tape recordings produces new and interesting sounds. He developed aleatory music—that is, music in which chance plays a large part. Basing his methods on the Chinese gambling game of I-Ching, Cage threw Chinese dice to decide which materials to use for his music and in what order. In *Water Music* a solo pianist is required to riffle a pack of cards, pour water from one container to another, and induce static from a radio set. *Imaginary Landscape No 4* has its sounds provided by twelve radio sets tuned at random, with two players to each set. Cage's love of silence is shown by *Four Minutes Thirty-three Seconds,* in three movements, during which the performer or performers make no noise at all.

MAIN COMPOSITIONS orchestral (including electronic effects); concrete music; piano works; works for prepared piano; chamber music; vocal music; audio-visual music.

31

CAMPION, THOMAS (1567–1620), an English physician, poet and dramatist, whose name is sometimes spelled *Campian*, is remembered for his songs with lute accompaniment, and for his treatises on musical theory. He wrote a number of books of lyric verse, books of songs, and several masques. His music, settings of his own words, is both delicate and charming. He practised as a doctor in London from about 1606.

MAIN COMPOSITIONS: *A Booke of Ayres* (words by Campion, music by Campion and Philip Rosseter 1601), *Two Bookes of Ayres* (1613), *The Third and Fourth Booke of Ayres* (1617), *A New Way of Making Fowre-Parts in Counter-point* (c. 1617).

CARISSIMI, GIACOMO (1605–74), an Italian musical director, was one of the earliest and most important developers of the oratorio and of the sacred cantata. After appointments at Tivoli and Assisi, he became *maestro di cappella* at the church of S Apollinare, Rome, where he spent the rest of his life. In his cantatas he developed the technique of recitative, and wrote light and varied orchestral accompaniments for his singers. His many oratorios were written for performance during Lent, when operas—already popular in Italy—were forbidden.

MAIN COMPOSITIONS 16 oratorios, including *Jephtha, Jonah, Baltazar*; Masses; cantatas; motets.

CAVALLI, (PIETRO) FRANCESCO (1602–76), was the pupil and assistant of CLAUDIO MONTEVERDI at St Mark's, Venice. He was born at Crema, in northern Italy, and his surname was originally Caletti-Bruni. He took the name of Cavalli in honour of his patron, Federigo Cavalli. In 1617 he became a singer at St Mark's, where Monteverdi was *maestro di cappella*, and subsequently became organist. At first his compositions were all for the Church, but in 1639 he composed the first of his many operas, which were to make his reputation. This work, *Le Nozze di Tetide e Peleo*, was the first to which the title 'opera' was given.

Cavalli's music owes much to the example and training of his great teacher. His operas are brilliant works in which the music is designed to follow the drama of the story-line very closely. His work for the theatre kept him busy, with visits to Paris and Innsbruck to produce operas for royal occasions, but he still found time to become *maestro di cappella* of St Mark's in 1668. The popularity of his operas, which were performed all over Italy, made him a rich man. Most of them have remained unheard ever since his death, though manuscripts of most of them still exist in Venice.

MAIN COMPOSITIONS: 42 operas, including *Le Nozze di Tetide e Peleo* (1639), *La Didone* (1641), *L'Egisto* (1643), *Il Giasone* (1649), *Serse* (1660), *Ercole amante* (1662); Church music.

CHERUBINI, (MARIA) LUIGI (CARLO ZENOBIO SAL-VATORE) (1760–1842), an Italian-born musician, spent much of his life in Paris. There he did a great deal to build up the newly-formed Paris conservatory, and was one of the first composers of romantic opera.

Cherubini's musical life fell into three periods. In the first period, up to 1780, he wrote mostly Church music. He then wrote the first of his thirty operas, and from 1784 to 1786 he was in London, during which time he spent a year as composer to King George III. After that he moved to Paris, which was to be his home, apart from a few short breaks, for the rest of his life. His opera period which lasted until 1816 brought him many disappointments, and his naturally gloomy mind became embittered. Then he was appointed joint musician to the French Chapel Royal, and turned his attention once more to Church music.

His conservative approach produced music of a somewhat severe and pure style, and he could not appreciate the comparatively unruly styles of LUDWIG VAN BEETHOVEN or HECTOR BERLIOZ—though Beethoven much admired Cherubini's vocal music.

MAIN COMPOSITIONS Church music: at least 8 Masses,

*Kyries,* cantatas, antiphons, oratorios; operas; orchestral: symphony (1815); chamber music.

CHOPIN, FRÉDÉRIC FRANÇOIS (1810–49), a Polish-French pianist, did a great deal both in his playing and his compositions to extend and improve the technique of piano-playing. His father, Nicolas Chopin, was a Frenchman from Lorraine who settled in Poland, became a tutor of French to a noble family near Warsaw, and married a Polish girl. Chopin's musical gifts developed early, and he gave his first public concert at the age of nine. Ten years of training and study passed before he made his real début, at a concert in Vienna. A second trip to Vienna a year later coincided with a Polish revolt against the Russians. Warsaw was occupied by Russian troops, and after some hesitation Chopin made his way to Paris, where he settled down as a teacher and composer, making a high income from pupils among the French aristocracy.

When he was twenty-six Chopin first met the novelist George Sand. This extraordinary woman, whose real name was Aurore Dudevant, was separated from her husband. She was a champion of women's rights, and a free-thinker who had many lovers. She was almost six years older than Chopin. After some months she and Chopin formed a liaison, and decided to go to Majorca, where they thought the climate would be good for Chopin's health, which was beginning to break up, and for the health of George Sand's young son, Maurice. But bad weather and bad accommodation did more to undermine Chopin's health than to build it up. For several years the two stayed together, spending the winters in Paris and the summers in George Sand's home in the country. During this time Chopin produced a steady flow of great compositions, while his health gradually grew worse. But the association finally broke up as a result of a series of quarrels in which George Sand's two children, Maurice and Solange, played a large part. Chopin, for all that he was a dandy with delicate, aristocratic ways, had a temper, and played his share in their disputes.

In 1848 the French king, Louis Philippe, was deposed and a republic was proclaimed. Chopin's social world collapsed, leaving him with no pupils and no income. In despair, he undertook a tour of England and Scotland, but the British weather did his tuberculosis no good, and he crept back to Paris a dying man.

Chopin's playing was easy and elegant, but on occasions possessed of a rugged strength. He could play his own works —which present many difficulties for the pianist—with effortless ease. He wrote many mazurkas and polonaises for the piano based on Polish melodies, and developed the nocturne, a piano piece devised by JOHN FIELD.

MAIN COMPOSITIONS piano and orchestra: two concertos; piano solos: 27 études, 51 mazurkas, 25 preludes, 19 nocturnes, 12 polonaises, 14 waltzes, sonatas and other works.

COPLAND, AARON (born 1900), an American pianist and composer, did much to create a distinctive American style of music, not just by the use of folk music themes, but by following up the natural idiom inherent in those tunes. He began his musical career late, having his first lessons at the age of fourteen. When he was twenty-one he went to Paris to study with NADIA BOULANGER, one of the greatest teachers of the twentieth century. His early music attracted much attention, and the help of a patron who financed him to allow him time to compose.

During his late twenties and early thirties Copland wrote a number of pieces of music in the more advanced style then becoming popular with American composers, music that appealed to the intellect much more than to the ear. But he realised that a gulf was opening between composers and listeners, and adopted a style which combined the freshness of modern harmonic freedoms, the tradition of American folk idiom, and a simplicity that made it easy to follow. At this time Copland wrote music for radio, children, and films. His ballet *Appalachian Spring* and the opera *The Tender Land* are particularly full of American idiom. In his later years

Copland produced a wide range of works, both orchestral and vocal, and some chamber music.

MAIN COMPOSITIONS operas: *The Second Hurricane* (1937), *The Tender Land* (1954); ballets: *Billy the Kid* (1938), *Rodeo* (1942), *Appalachian Spring* (1944); orchestral: symphonies, overtures, concertos for clarinet and piano, suites; piano music; songs and song cycles; chamber music. BOOKS *What to Listen for in Music* (1937), *Our New Music* (1941), *Music and Imagination* (1952), *Copland on Music* (1960).

CORELLI, ARCHANGELO (1653–1713), an Italian, was one of the first important player-composer-teacher violinists. After travelling in Germany he settled in Rome at the home of his friend and patron, Cardinal Pietro Ottoboni, where he conducted weekly concerts. His skill as a violinist brought him pupils from all over Europe. He lived simply, collecting pictures and amassing a considerable fortune. As a composer he laid the foundations of violin writing at a time when the violin was ousting the viol as the main stringed instrument.

MAIN COMPOSITIONS 4 sets of 12 sonatas for two violins and continuo; 12 sonatas for violin and continuo; 12 concerti grossi.

COUPERIN, FRANÇOIS (1668–1733), was the greatest of a large French family of musicians who lived in Paris between 1626 and 1850. He is often called *Couperin le Grand* to distinguish him from his many relations. He succeeded his father as organist of the church of St Gervais, Paris, when he was only eleven, but a deputy performed the duties of the post until Couperin was old enough to take over. Later he was organist to the Chapel Royal of Louis XIV, and teacher of Louis's children.

Couperin is best remembered for his harpsichord pieces. Most of them are short, and bear titles descriptive of their music, such as *The Enchantress* or *Bacchanalian Passion*. He wrote an important treatise on harpsichord playing, *L'art de toucher le clavecin*.

MAIN COMPOSITIONS harpsichord pieces (4 volumes); organ music; Church music; chamber music, including two sonatas; songs.

DALLAPICCOLA, LUIGI (born 1904), an Italian pianist and teacher, was the first important Italian composer to adopt the twelve-tone system of composition. Dallapiccola had a very difficult life; he was born in a region then under Austrian rule, and on the outbreak of World War I his family and other Italians of the area were imprisoned, then deported to Graz, in Austria. After the war they returned to Italy, and Dallapiccola studied in Florence. His early compositions were advanced in style—too advanced for the Fascist government then in power, which favoured 'traditional' music. His dislike of the régime intensified when the Fascists adopted an anti-Jewish policy and dismissed Dallapiccola's Jewish-born wife from her job in Florence's National Library.

When the Nazi German forces occupied Florence during World War II Dallapiccola had to go into hiding. During this time he produced his first work on the twelve-tone system, the song-cycle *Sex Carmina Alcaei*. His sufferings and those of his country inspired him with thoughts of freedom, and led to his great one-act opera *Il Prigioniero* (*The Prisoner*). His later works, while cast in the twelve-tone mould, show many other influences, particularly a Romantic streak.

MAIN COMPOSITIONS operas: *Volo di Notte* (1940), *Il Prigioniero* (1949), *Ulysses* (1968); ballet *Marsia* (1943); orchestral music, including pieces with violin, piano, soprano, and baritone solo; chamber music; choral music; songs and song cycles.

DEBUSSY, (ACHILLE) CLAUDE (1862–1918), a French pianist and composer, founded the so-called 'Impressionist' style of writing music, avoiding dramatic and formal music and writing pieces in which the emphasis was on variations of tone and harmony. The son of a former marine, Debussy was intended for the sea. But his great musical gifts were discovered when he was ten, and he at once entered the Paris conservatory, where he studied for 11 years.

Debussy was influenced by the music of Russia (to which he paid a visit), RICHARD WAGNER, and plainsong, and even more strongly by the 'symbolist' poetry of Stéphane Mallarmé and the paintings of Renoir, Gauguin, and others. He wrote a prelude based on Mallarmé's poem 'L'Après-midi d'un faune'. His only opera, *Pelléas et Mélisande*, was a setting of Maurice Maeterlinck's atmospheric tragedy. Debussy was poor for most of his life. A shy man, he rarely appeared in public and held no official posts.

MAIN COMPOSITIONS opera *Pelléas et Mélisande* (1902); ballets: *Jeux* (1913), *Khamma* (1924), *La Boîte à joujoux* (unfinished); orchestral: suite, *Printemps*, tone-poems *Prélude à L'Après-midi d'un faune* (1894), *La Mer* (1905), *Images* (1906–9); chamber music; many piano solos, including preludes and studies; choral works; songs.

DELIBES, (CLEMENT PHILIBERT) LÉO (1836–91), a French organist and pianist, composed a number of operas, operettas, and ballets. His most famous works are the ballets *Sylvia* and *Coppélia*, and the opera *Lakmé* which includes the 'Bell Song', a showpiece much loved by coloratura sopranos. His first appointment was as accompanist at the Théâtre Lyrique, and later he became accompanist and chorus master at the Paris Opéra. For some years he also held appointments as a church organist. His first successes were with operettas. Then he was asked to collaborate with the Russian Ludwig Minkus to write the music for the ballet *La Source*. His work was so much better than that of Minkus that he was asked to write more ballets. But he then returned to opera, which he preferred. His music is light, graceful, and polished.

MAIN COMPOSITIONS ballets: *La Source* (in part, 1866), *Coppélia* (1870), *Sylvia* (1876); operas: *Le Roi l'a dit* (1873), *Jean de Nivelle* (1880), *Lakmé* (1883); operettas; songs.

DELIUS, FREDERICK (1862–1934), a British composer of Dutch-German ancestry, produced music that was quite unlike anyone else's—romantic, atmospheric, and full of subtle and unexpected shifts of harmony. His father was a woollen merchant and wanted his son to become a businessman. For a time Delius was an orange planter in Florida, but he spent most of his time on music. Eventually, through the persuasion of his friend EDVARD GRIEG, he won permission and funds to study music. From 1901 he spent most of his time on a small estate at Grez-sur-Loing, a village in north-central France. In the 1920s he became blind and paralysed, but continued to dictate his compositions to an amanuensis. He is best remembered for his short lyrical pieces for orchestra, such as *On Hearing the First Cuckoo in Spring,* and 'The Walk to the Paradise Garden' from the opera *A Village Romeo and Juliet.*

MAIN COMPOSITIONS operas: *A Village Romeo and Juliet* (1907), *Irmelin* (1953), *Koanga* (1904), *Fennimore and Gerda* (1919); orchestral: *In a Summer Garden, On Hearing the First Cuckoo in Spring, Summer Night on the River, Song Before Sunrise, Eventyr, Paris, Brigg Fair,* concertos for violin, cello, piano; chorus and orchestra: *Appalachia, Sea Drift, A Mass of Life, A Song of the High Hills;* unaccompanied choral works; chamber music; songs.

D'INDY, (PAUL MARIE THÉODORE) VINCENT (1851–1931), a French organist, conductor, and teacher, was a devoted follower of CÉSAR FRANCK. As well as being influenced by Franck, he also came under the spell of RICHARD WAGNER.

After distinguished military service during the Franco-Prussian War of 1870–1, d'Indy devoted himself to study, meanwhile earning his living as an orchestral player. Later, he helped to found a school of music in Paris, the Schola Cantorum, and devoted his efforts to building up a new school of French composition based on classical and plainsong traditions. He helped to revive the works of CLAUDIO MONTEVERDI, and also revived works by J. S. BACH and other eighteenth-century composers. His breadth of view, however, also made him a champion of CLAUDE DEBUSSY, whose music was not in accordance with d'Indy's theories. D'Indy's own compositions are thoughtfully written, and reflect his great love of nature. He was an enthusiastic collector of folk-songs.

MAIN COMPOSITIONS operas: *Attendez-moi sous l'orme* (1882), *Le Chant de la cloche* (1886), *Fervaal* (1897), *L'Étranger* (1903), *La Légende de St Christophe* (1920), *Le Rêve de Cinyras* (1927); orchestral: 3 symphonies, one for piano and orchestra; chamber music; religious and secular choral works; songs; folk-song arrangements.

DOHNÁNYI, ERNÖ (1877–1960), was a Hungarian pianist and conductor. He began touring as a pianist while a young man, and was acclaimed as one of the world's leading players. For many years he taught the piano at the Berlin conservatory, and then settled in Budapest, where he held various leading posts as a teacher and conductor. His views made him unacceptable to the post-war Communist government, and in 1949 he settled in the United States. His best-known work is his *Variations on a Nursery Song* for piano and orchestra. His piano works are particularly admired.

MAIN COMPOSITIONS operas: *Tante Simona* (1913), *A Vajda Tornya* (1922), *A Tenor* (1929); ballet: *Der Schleier der Pierette* (1910); orchestral: 3 symphonies, *Variations on a Nursery Song* (piano and orchestra, 1934), violin concerto; chamber music; piano solos; songs.

DONIZETTI, (DOMENICO) GAETANO (MARIA) (1797–1848), was a prolific Italian composer of operas, of which he produced seventy. His parents opposed his taking up a career in opera, so he joined the Austrian army, composing in his spare time. In 1822 the success of his opera *Zoraide di Granata*, produced in Venice, procured him exemption from further military service. He worked mainly in Milan and Naples until 1838, when he moved to Paris after the death of his young wife, Virginia. There he won a great success with the light opera *La Fille du régiment*. His last opera, *Catarina Cornaro*, was produced in Naples in 1844. He wrote many of his own librettos.

The final years of Donizetti's life were tragic. He became subject to fits of melancholy, which gradually led to insanity and paralysis.

MAIN COMPOSITIONS 70 operas including *Enrico di Borgogna* (1818), *Anna Bolena* (1830), *L'Elisir d'Amore* (1832), *Lucrezia Borgia* and *Torquato Tasso* (1833), *Lucia di Lammermoor* (1835), *La Fille du régiment* (1840), *La Favorite* (1840), *Linda di Chamounix* (1842), *Don Pasquale* (1843), *Caterina Cornaro* (1844).


DOWLAND, JOHN (1562–1626), an English composer, was known in his own time as an outstanding lutenist. Little is known of his early life, but he was probably born in Ireland, and was a Roman Catholic. He set out on an extensive European tour in the 1590s, which ended in an appointment as lutenist to the Danish king at a salary that can only be described as princely. A tendency to overspend and to overstay his periods of leave led to his dismissal in 1606, and he returned to England, eventually securing a post as lutenist to King James I. He is now remembered for his many songs and lute pieces. His music is noted for its gentle melancholy.

MAIN COMPOSITIONS 4 *Bookes of Songs or Ayres* (1597, 1600, 1603, 1612); *Lachrymae* for lute, viols, or violins (1605).


DUFAY, GUILLERMUS (*c.* 1400–74), a Belgian Church singer and canon, was one of the finest composers of his day, both of Church music and secular music. He began his career as a chorister at Cambrai Cathedral, in northern France, and later became a singer in the papal choir at Rome and elsewhere. He spent several years in Savoy, and was also in the service of the Duke of Burgundy. His last thirty years were spent back at Cambrai, where he was appointed a canon.

Dufay was just one—but the greatest—of the many singers from the Low Countries who served in the papal choir.

His style was graceful, and he was strongly influenced by the English composer JOHN DUNSTABLE.

MAIN COMPOSITIONS Masses and other Church music; songs and motets.

DUKAS, PAUL ABRAHAM (1865–1935), a French teacher and editor, is remembered for one work, *L'Apprenti Sorcier*, a lively piece of programme music. From 1910 until his death he was a professor at the Paris conservatory—for most of the time teaching composition. In 1912 he stopped publishing his works, except for two small pieces. He kept on writing music, but shortly before his death he burnt all his manuscripts.

MAIN COMPOSITIONS opera *Ariane et Barbe-Bleue* (1907); ballet *La Péri* (1912); orchestral: 1 symphony (1896), programme music, including *L'Apprenti Sorcier* (1897); piano music; songs.

DUNSTABLE, JOHN (*c.* 1385–1453), an English musician, astronomer, and mathematician, had an enormous influence on the music of continental Europe, and especially on the music of the Low Countries—the Netherlands and Belgium. Almost nothing is known of his life, except that he may have been born at Dunstable, in Bedfordshire, and that he spent some while in the service of John, Duke of Bedford, Henry VI's uncle, who was regent of France. Dunstable almost certainly spent some time in France, as he wrote music for Henry's coronation in that country. He died in London. Dunstable's strong influence on his European contemporaries, such as GUILLERMUS DUFAY, arose from his mastery of counterpoint, and his innovations in harmony. Copies of his music have been found in collections in Italy, suggesting that he may have been there for a time.

MAIN COMPOSITIONS Masses, motets, songs.

DVOŘÁK, ANTONÍN (1841–1904), a Bohemian violinist, organist, and teacher, was one of the finest Czech composers.

He was born not far from Prague, the son of an innkeeper, in an area where music-making was a common and natural thing. Dvořák studied at an organ school in Prague for two years, then worked as a teacher and played the viola in an orchestra for ten years, working away at composition in his spare time. Eventually his music brought him to the notice of influential musicians such as the violinist Joseph Joachim, and JOHANNES BRAHMS. With their aid he began to publish his music, and won international recognition.

After visits to England, where his choral works particularly were a great success, Dvořák became professor of composition at the Prague conservatory. Then, when he was fifty-one, he was appointed director of the National Conservatory of Music in New York City. Dvořák himself gained most from the three years he spent there—his ability as a teacher was not particularly high. Two of his most famous compositions date from his American stay: the symphony *From the New World,* and the string quartet opus 97, originally nicknamed the *Nigger* and now generally called the *American* quartet. Both these works have themes that owe something to American folk music, though they are unmistakably Bohemian in character. But Dvořák missed his homeland, and in 1895 he returned to Prague and a quietly busy life of teaching and composing.

MAIN COMPOSITIONS 9 operas, including *The Jacobin* (1889), *The Devil and Kate* (1899), *Rusalka* (1901); orchestral: 9 symphonies, overtures, symphonic poems, concertos for piano, violin, cello; choral: *Stabat Mater* (1877), *Te Deum* (1892); chamber music: quartets, piano trios; piano solos; songs.

ELGAR, SIR EDWARD WILLIAM (1857–1934), a violinist and teacher, became the leading English composer of the early 1900s. He was the son of a music dealer and organist. He left school at the age of fifteen, and after a spell in a lawyer's office devoted his life to music. Besides the violin he played the piano, organ, cello, double-bass, bassoon, and trombone. His earliest conducting post was with the staff orchestra at a lunatic asylum. He spent much time composing from an early stage in his career, and gradually won fame for his works. His reputation grew on music designed especially for choral societies.

Elgar came to the forefront of English musical life in 1899 with the *Enigma Variations* for orchestra, containing musical 'portraits' of his friends. Soon afterwards he became the favourite composer of King Edward VII, who rewarded his genius with a knighthood. In 1920 Elgar suffered a severe blow with the death of his wife, from which he never fully recovered.

Elgar's music is full of memorable melodies, richly orchestrated. An example is the patriotic song 'Land of Hope and Glory', which is an arrangement of a theme from one of his *Pomp and Circumstance* marches.

MAIN COMPOSITIONS orchestral: 2 symphonies, *Enigma Variations* (1899), overture *Cockaigne* (1901), 5 *Pomp and Circumstance* marches (1901–5), *Introduction and Allegro for Strings* (1905), suites *The Wand of Youth* (1907–8), concertos for violin and cello; choral: oratorios *The Dream of Gerontius* (1900), *The Apostles* (1903), *The Kingdom* (1906); other choral works including *The Black Knight* (1893), *Lux Christi* (1896), *King Olaf* (1896), *The Music Makers* (1912); ballets and incidental music for plays; chamber music; songs.

FALLA, MANUEL DE (1876–1946), Spain's principal musician in the first part of the 1900s, came to fame with his music for the ballet *The Three-Cornered Hat,* a witty and lively work. Falla studied the piano in Madrid, and later taught it in Paris. He returned to Madrid in 1914 when World War I broke out. In 1926 he retired to Majorca, and in 1939, after the Spanish Civil War, he moved to Argentina, where he spent his remaining years in poor health. He was deeply interested in the folk songs of southern Spain, which influenced his work.

MAIN COMPOSITIONS operas: *La Vida Breve (Life is Short*

1905), *Master Peter's Puppet Show* (1923), *Alantida* (completed by Ernst Halffter, 1961); ballets: *Wedded by Witchcraft* (1915), *The Three-Cornered Hat* (1919); orchestral: suite *Nights in the Gardens of Spain,* for piano and orchestra (1916), harpsichord concerto (1926); chamber music; songs.

FAURÉ, GABRIEL URBAIN (1845–1924), a French organist and teacher, is especially known for his songs and his chamber music, though his larger-scale music is also much performed, particularly his Requiem Mass. Fauré held a succession of Church musical posts. In 1896 he became organist at La Madeleine, in Paris, and also professor of composition at the Paris conservatory. Later he became director of the conservatory. Deafness forced him to retire at the age of seventy-five.

Fauré's teaching brought an atmosphere of freshness into the Paris conservatory, where his pupils included MAURICE RAVEL. His own numerous compositions are distinguished by daring harmonies and other innovations, all disguised by an appearance of classical style and elegance.

MAIN COMPOSITIONS Requiem Mass (1888); operas: *Prométhée* (1900), *Pénélope* (1913); incidental music for plays, including *Pélleas et Mélisande* (1898); orchestral music, including a symphony; Church music; piano: nocturnes, barcarolles, impromptus; other chamber music; many songs.

FIELD, JOHN (1782–1837), an Irish pianist who spent much of his life in Russia, is remembered chiefly for having devised the slow, romantic piano piece known as the *nocturne,* later developed by FRÉDÉRIC CHOPIN. Field was apprenticed in London to the Italian pianist and pianomaker Muzio Clementi who taught him. Clementi used Field to demonstrate and sell his pianos all over Europe. Field eventually settled in St Petersburg (Leningrad), in Russia.

MAIN COMPOSITIONS 7 piano concertos; rondos, polonaises and nocturnes for piano; other chamber music.

FINZI, GERALD (1901–56), was widely regarded as one of the leading British song-writers of his day. His skill lay in his ability to interpret the mood and thought of the poets whose works he set, ranging from William Shakespeare to Thomas Hardy. He had a lonely and unhappy childhood, but decided to be a composer at the early age of nine. As a young man he did not make friends readily, and became shy and withdrawn—a state from which his marriage rescued him in 1933. This marriage came at the end of three years as professor of composition at the Royal Academy of Music, London, his only formal musical post.

Finzi worked slowly, taking as long as twenty-five years to complete some of his works. Though he was an energetic and insatiably curious man, he would not hurry composition if it would not 'come right' immediately.

MAIN COMPOSITIONS orchestral: *Introit* for violin and orchestra; voice and orchestra: cantata *Dies Natalis* (1939), *Ode for St Cecilia's Day* (1947), *In Terra Pax* (1954); songs; song cycle, *Let Us Garlands Bring* (1942).


FOSTER, STEPHEN COLLINS (1826–64), was for many years regarded as 'the people's composer' in the United States because of the quantity of songs he wrote that have become evergreen favourites. Foster was born near Pittsburg, Pennsylvania, and taught himself to play the flageolet when a small boy. Though he had no formal musical education, he began to write songs, and made his first hit with *Oh! Susanna* in 1848. Much of his music was inspired by Negro melodies, perhaps heard from plantation workers, but more likely from minstrel shows. Many of his songs were commissioned for such shows. Foster made a great deal of money from his work, but died a comparatively poor man.

Among the most famous of his 175 songs are *My Old Kentucky Home*, *Swanee Ribber*, *Old Black Joe*, *Camptown Races*, *Massa's in de Cold, Cold Ground*, *Jeanie With the Light Brown Hair* and *Beautiful Dreamer*. He wrote the words of nearly all his songs.

MAIN COMPOSITIONS 175 songs; choral and instrumental works.

FRANCK, CÉSAR AUGUSTE JEAN GUILLAUME HUBERT (1822–90), a Belgian-born French organist and teacher, has been much more revered as a composer since his death than he was during his lifetime. He studied first at Liège, his birthplace. His father, a banker, then moved to Paris to give his son a chance to go to the conservatory there. Franck became a church organist in Paris at the age of twenty-eight and remained in the service of the Church until his death. He was made organ professor at the conservatory at the age of fifty. Franck's improvisations at the organ were greatly admired.

He led a simple, well-ordered life. When he was sixty-eight he scored what he regarded as his first real success as a composer, when his string quartet was warmly applauded. A month later he was injured in a street accident, and died a few months after. Franck's musical style is both sweet and rich, with a great deal of light and shade in it. Much of his best work was written towards the end of his life, at a period when he had to rise at 5am each day in order to find time for composition before his busy round of teaching began.

MAIN COMPOSITIONS operas: *Le Valet de ferme* (1852), *Hulda* (1894), *Ghisèle* (1896); oratorios: *Ruth* (1845), *Rédemption* (1872), *Rebecca* (1879), *Les Béatitudes* (1879); other Church music and choral works; orchestral: symphony, works for piano and orchestra; chamber music; piano and organ solos; songs.

GABRIELI, ANDREA (*c* 1510–86), a Venetian organist and singer, was trained by Adrian Willaert, one of the many Flemish musicians then resident in Italy. After travelling in central Europe Gabrieli returned to Venice. There he became an organist at St Mark's Basilica, where he remained. He was famous for his madrigals, and for his organ compositions. He was one of the first composers of fugues, and of

47

works for double choir. The most famous of his many pupils was his nephew GIOVANNI GABRIELI.

MAIN COMPOSITIONS sonatas for five instruments (1586); sacred songs for five voices (1565); canzoni for organ (1571); *Penitential Psalms* (1583); cantatas; Masses; madrigals; organ pieces.

GABRIELI, GIOVANNI (1557–1612), a Venetian organist, was the nephew and pupil of ANDREA GABRIELI. He studied in Venice and Munich, where he had lessons from ORLANDO DI LASSO. In 1584 he succeeded his uncle as second organist at St Mark's, Venice. In addition to writing works for voices which could also be played on instruments, as the custom then was, he wrote for instruments alone, and was one of the first composers to use the term *sonata* for an instrumental work. In his religious compositions he pioneered the use of a more emotional approach, as distinct from the austere, other-worldly Church music of the Middle Ages, which was based on plainsong.

MAIN COMPOSITIONS *Sacrae symphoniae* (1597); choral works; madrigals; organ music.

GEMINIANI, FRANCESCO (1687–1762), an Italian violinist, wrote an important early work on violin-playing. He was a brilliant soloist, but a poor conductor and leader for an orchestra. After holding posts in Lucca and Naples, Geminiani went to England in 1714. There he established himself as a teacher and soloist. A passion for dealing in pictures, about which he knew little, led him to a debtors' prison, from which one of his rich pupils rescued him. He produced many works for the violin, which his contemporaries found too difficult to play. Among his many theoretical writings was *The Art of Playing the Violin*, still valuable as a guide to the musical style of the day. He died during a visit to one of his pupils in Dublin.

MAIN COMPOSITIONS concertos, solos, and sonatas for violin; concerti grossi; trios.

GERMAN, SIR EDWARD (1862–1936), was second only to
SIR ARTHUR SULLIVAN as a British composer of light operas.
His real name was *Edward German Jones*, but he dropped
the Jones when he adopted music as his profession. His first
job was playing the violin in a theatre orchestra, but he soon
became a conductor. He put his knowledge of the theatre to
good use as a writer of incidental music for plays, and the
three dances he wrote for William Shakespeare's *Henry VIII*
became instantly popular, remaining so ever since.

German began his career as a writer of light operas by completing *The Emerald Isle*, left unfinished by Sullivan when
he died. The following year German wrote *Merrie England*,
to a text by Basil Hood, who had written the libretto of *The
Emerald Isle*. Although the words have often been criticised
as inferior to the music, *Merrie England* has remained consistently popular. But *Fallen Fairies*, to words by W. S.
Gilbert, is now forgotten. German was knighted in 1928.

MAIN COMPOSITIONS light operas: *Merrie England* (1902),
*A Princess of Kensington* (1903), *Tom Jones* (1907), *Fallen
Fairies* (1909); orchestral: symphonies, suites, rhapsodies;
songs.

GERSHWIN, GEORGE (1898–1937), an American jazz
pianist, was one of the first composers to bridge the gap
between serious and popular music. After writing a number
of popular songs and musical comedies, Gershwin produced
in 1924 his *Rhapsody in Blue,* a one-movement concerto for
piano and orchestra. Its success led him to produce several
other works for piano and orchestra, and a symphonic poem,
*An American in Paris* (1928). His greatest work was the
Negro folk-opera *Porgy and Bess*.

MAIN COMPOSITIONS works for piano and orchestra: *Rhapsody in Blue* (1924), concerto in F (1925), *Three Piano Preludes* (1926), *Second Rhapsody* (1932), *Cuban Overture*
(1934); orchestral: *An American in Paris* (1928); operas:
*Blue Monday*, or *135th Street* (1923), *Porgy and Bess* (1935);
musicals: *La, La, Lucille* (1920), *Lady Be Good* (1924), *Tip*

49

D

*Toes* (1925), *Oh Kay!* (1926), *Funny Face* (1927), *Strike Up the Band* (1929), *Girl Crazy* (1930), *Of Thee I Sing* (1932); film scores.

## GESUALDO, CARLO, PRINCE OF VENOSA (*c.* 1560–1613), an Italian nobleman, wrote six sets of madrigals whose harmonies were far in advance of any others of the time. In 1590 he had his first wife murdered, having caught her with a lover (who was also killed). Despite all this violence—not uncommon in the Italy of his day—he was an elegant, fastidious man, passionately fond of music, and a virtuoso performer on the lute.

MAIN COMPOSITIONS 6 books of madrigals (1594–1611); *Responsoriae* (1611); sacred songs (1603).

## GIBBONS, ORLANDO (1583–1625), an English organist, was the most distinguished member of a large musical family. His father, three of his brothers, and one of his sons were also active musicians. Orlando Gibbons began his career as a boy chorister at King's College, Cambridge University. At the age of twenty-one he became organist of the Chapel Royal, where he remained for the rest of his days. For the last two years of his life he was also organist of Westminster Abbey. He died of apoplexy while attending King Charles I at Canterbury to meet his bride-to-be, Princess Henrietta Maria of France. Gibbons is renowned for his madrigals and Church music, and in his prime was unrivalled in England as a keyboard player. Among his many madrigals is the ever-popular 'The Silver Swan'.

MAIN COMPOSITIONS 2 Church services, *Te Deum* and *Jubilate*; more than 30 anthems; hymns; madrigals and motets; fantasias for strings; almans, corantos, galliards, and ayres for keyboard.

## GLAZUNOV, ALEKSANDR KONSTANTINOVICH (1865–1936), was a Russian music teacher and symphonist. Although he studied with MILI BALAKIREV and NIKOLAI RIM-

SKY-KORSAKOV, his work was more influenced by the composers of western Europe, particularly JOHANNES BRAHMS, than by the traditional music of his own country. He wrote the first of his eight symphonies when he was only sixteen. It was performed the following year under the direction of Balakirev, and was much admired. A revised version was published by a rich timber merchant, Mitrofan Belaief, who was so inspired by the work that he started a publishing company to produce the works of Russian writers.

Glazunov wrote most of his music before 1906, when he became director of the St Petersburg (Leningrad) conservatory. From then on he devoted his time largely to teaching. He spent his last years in Paris.

MAIN COMPOSITIONS orchestral: 8 symphonies, symphonic poem *Stenka Razin* (1885), overtures, suites, 2 piano concertos, 2 violin concertos, concerto-ballata for cello; ballets: *Raymonda, Ruses d'amour, Les Saisons;* chamber music: 7 string quartets; choral music; piano solos.

GLINKA, MIKHAIL IVANOVICH (1804–57), a Russian civil servant and man of independent means, was one of the first great Russian composers. He heard much Russian folk music on his wealthy father's estate, but began to study music seriously after hearing a private orchestra maintained by his uncle. For a time he had piano lessons from JOHN FIELD. He joined the civil service when aged twenty, but gave up his post after four years because of ill-health and a lack of ambition.

Glinka went to Italy to recover, and came under the spell of the opera writers VINCENZO BELLINI and GAETANO DONIZETTI. Realising his lack of technical skill, he devoted himself to a spell of hard study, and then returned to Russia, where he married and settled down. In 1836 he produced his first opera, *Ivan Susanin,* better known by its alternative title *A Life for the Tsar.* This opera had a Russian text and Russian and Polish melodies, and its strongly patriotic theme won Glinka a post at court as Master of the Imperial Chapel. His second opera, *Ruslan and Ludmilla,* a fairy-tale with oriental settings, proved less popular, but it had a great influence on later Russian composers. He spent much of his later life roaming about Europe.

MAIN COMPOSITIONS operas: *Ivan Susanin* (*A Life for the Tsar*, 1836), *Ruslan and Ludmilla* (1842); orchestral music; choral works; chamber music; piano solos; songs.

GLUCK, CHRISTOPH WILLIBALD (1714–87), a Bavarian forester's son—possibly of Czech ancestry—led a change in opera from a series of artificial stories about gods and goddesses, designed mainly to show off the singers' voices, to dramas about ordinary people, with a strong sense of theatre. After a childhood spent running wild in the forests near his home he was sent to a Jesuit school, where he learned music among his other studies. At the age of eighteen he went to Prague, where he supported himself by singing and playing the cello, while continuing his studies. When he was twenty-two he went to Vienna, and there a wealthy Italian, Prince Melzi, asked Gluck to join his private orchestra in Milan.

In Milan Gluck studied composition and began to write music, and after four years produced his first opera, *Artaserse*. It was based on a libretto by the popular Italian poet Pietro Metastasio, and was a typical formal Italian opera of its day. He continued to write operas of this kind, and might have done so all his days had he not been invited to visit London, where he came under the influence of GEORGE FRIDERIC HANDEL. Handel was scathing about Gluck ('He knows no more of counterpoint than my cook'), but helped him considerably.

Gluck decided to change his ways. He settled in Vienna, where he married a girl with some money. At some time during this period he was given a knighthood by the Pope, which entitled him to be called Ritter von Gluck. For a time he wrote music for French comedies, which were at least about realistic people. Then he had the good fortune to team up with a librettist, Raniero Calazabigi, who shared his ideas. In 1762 the two produced *Orfeo ed Euridice*, in which Gluck made great use of the chorus, and used the orchestra instead of just a harpsichord to accompany the solo recitatives—changes which caused a sensation and made a lot of money for Gluck. After several other works of varying style and merit, written to please audiences and patrons, he produced *Alceste*, one of his masterpieces. In a preface to the score he wrote: 'I have thought it necessary to reduce music to its true function, which is that of seconding poetry in the expression of the sentiments and dramatic situations of a story.'

One of Gluck's pupils in Vienna was a young princess, Marie Antoinette, who later married the dauphin (crown prince) of France. As a result he was invited to Paris, where he arrived at the age of fifty-nine. There his success was marred by a 'war' carried on in the newspapers between factions supporting his music and that of a traditional Italian composer, Niccolò Piccinni.

MAIN COMPOSITIONS 45 operas including *Artaserse* (1741), *Semiramide Riconosciuta* (1748), *Orfeo ed Euridice* (1762), *Alceste* (1767), *Paride ed Elena* (1770), *Iphigénie en Aulide* (1774), *Iphigénie en Tauride* (1778); ballets: *Alessandro* (1755), *L'Orfano della China* (1766), *Don Juan* (1761), *Semiramide* (1765); overtures; sonatas for two violins and bass; songs.

GOUNOD, CHARLES FRANÇOIS (1818–93), a French organist and choirmaster, is chiefly remembered for his opera *Faust*—a work so superior to his other compositions that some people doubted if he really wrote it. His mother, a professional pianist, was his first teacher, and he later studied at the Paris conservatory and won the Prix de Rome. He was deeply religious, and studied for the priesthood. But he abandoned the idea in 1847 and took up the composition of operas. *Faust*, produced when he was forty-one, was a triumph.

In 1870 Gounod moved to England, where he formed a choir which still survives as the Royal Choral Society. After five years he returned to France, where he devoted himself largely to oratorios and Church music. Among his smaller works his *Meditation* 'Ave Maria', using J. S. BACH's prelude in C major as accompaniment, has remained popular.

MAIN COMPOSITIONS 12 operas, including *Sappho* (1851), *Faust* (1859), *Roméo et Juliette* (1867), *Mireille* (1864); choral: oratorios, Masses and other Church music; orchestral: 2 symphonies; chamber music; piano solos; songs.

GRAINGER, PERCY ALDRIDGE (1882–1961), an Australian-born pianist, was best known for his work of collecting English folk songs, and for his hearty, open-air style of music. He delighted in writing all his musical instructions in English instead of Italian, using such terms as 'clatteringly' and 'louden lots'. He studied first in Melbourne, where he was born, and later in Germany, where he became a friend of EDVARD GRIEG. In 1914 he emigrated to the United States, and later became an American citizen. He spent his time playing, teaching, and composing. Always an extrovert, he celebrated his marriage to the Swedish poetess Ella Viola Ström in the Hollywood Bowl—a vast open-air theatre—in front of twenty thousand people, whom he entertained by conducting a concert of his own compositions.

Among Grainger's most popular works are a number of orchestral pieces based on folk tunes, such as *Shepherd's Hey* and *Country Gardens*, but he also wrote some more thoughtful works, particularly his chamber music. He founded the Percy Grainger Museum at Melbourne.

MAIN COMPOSITIONS orchestral: *Mock Morris* (1911), *Molly on the Shore* (1921), *Shepherd's Hey* (1922), *Country Gardens* (1925), *Handel in the Strand* (1930); chamber music.

GRANADOS, ENRIQUE (1867–1916), a pianist, was a leading Spanish composer. At the age of sixteen he was studying composition with Felipe Pedrell, founder of the Spanish nationalist tradition in music, while earning his living playing the piano in a restaurant. After two years' study in Paris he began his concert career in Spain and quickly established himself as a leading pianist. He founded a music school in

Barcelona, which produced many fine pianists, and began writing operas. Among his many piano works was a series of musical 'pictures' based on the paintings of Francisco Goya, which he called *Goyescas*. He later turned this into an opera, which had its first performance in New York in 1916, during World War I. Granados and his wife were drowned on their way home when the British cross-channel ship *Sussex*, in which they were travelling, was torpedoed by a German submarine. Their son, Edward, also a conductor and composer, took over the Barcelona music school.

MAIN COMPOSITIONS operas: *María del Carmen* (1898), *Petrarca* (1901), *Picarol* (1901), *Follet* (1903), *Gaziel* (1906), *Liliana* (1911), *Goyescas* (1916); piano solos including 12 *Danzas españolas* (1892); chamber music; songs.

GRIEG, EDVARD HAGERUP (1843–1907), Norway's greatest musician, was the great-grandson of Alexander Greig, a Jacobite who left Scotland after the defeat of Bonnie Prince Charlie at Culloden in 1746. His first teacher was his mother, from whom he inherited his musical gifts. At the age of fifteen he went to the Leipzig conservatory in Germany, where one of his fellow students was ARTHUR SULLIVAN. A serious illness while he was there cost him the use of one lung. Later he went to Copenhagen to study, and there met a fellow Norwegian, Rikard Nordraak, who introduced him to Norway's great heritage of folk music. From then on Grieg was dedicated to the cause of Norwegian music. At this time Norway was still politically united with Sweden, though nationalist movements were gaining ground.

Grieg found his task uphill work, and when he and his wife Nina—his cousin—lost their only child he felt the fates were against him. But an encouraging letter from, and a meeting with, FRANZ LISZT, then Europe's grand old man of music, spurred him on to fresh endeavours. When Grieg was thirty-one the Norwegian government awarded him a small state pension, which enabled him to live in the country and compose. He and Nina, who was a singer, made many concert tours of Europe, Grieg conducting and playing the piano.

Grieg's music is lyrical, and essentially Norwegian in mood and style. Much of his best work was for his own instrument, the piano, and his piano concerto is one of the most popular.

MAIN COMPOSITIONS incidental music to *Sigurd Jorsalfar* (1872), *Peer Gynt* (1875); orchestral: symphony, piano concerto, suites from *Peer Gynt* and *Sigurd Jorsalfar*; chamber music; piano solos; piano duets; choral works; songs.

HANDEL, GEORGE FRIDERIC (1685–1759), a German-born organist and impresario, became an English citizen and, with his exact contemporary JOHANN SEBASTIAN BACH, one of the two greatest composers of his time. Handel was the son of a barber-surgeon at Halle, in Saxony, and at his father's wish studied law at Halle University. But he had already set his heart on a musical career. While he was still studying law he held the post of organist at Halle Cathedral, and as soon as he left the university he went to Hamburg to play the violin in the opera house orchestra. While there he wrote his first opera, *Almira*, a nonsensical work sung partly in Italian and partly in German which nevertheless won immediate success for its fresh, lively music. Earlier, again like Bach, he had journeyed to Lübeck to see whether he could succeed DIETRICH BUXTEHUDE as organist of St Mary's. But because the job entailed marrying one of Buxtehude's five daughters, the plan came to nothing. During his stay in Hamburg Handel fought a duel with a fellow musician.

At the age of twenty-one Handel went to Italy, where he absorbed Italian style and influences, and wrote a number of operas which brought him widespread fame. They also brought him an appointment as *Kapellmeister* to the Elector George of Hanover. He obtained leave to visit England, where his operas again scored a success—so much so that in 1712 he obtained leave once again and returned to England. This time he prospered so well that he forgot, or neglected, to return to his duties in Hanover. He was soon acknowledged as London's leading musician, and was awarded a state pension by Queen Anne.

In 1714 Anne died, to be succeeded as England's sovereign by Handel's neglected employer, the Elector George. Handel soon made his peace with King George—according to an unconfirmed story, by composing a suite of music that was played to the king while he was holding a water-party on the River Thames. This was the famous *Water Music,* parts of which were certainly written about this time. Soon afterwards Handel retired for a time from the opera scene in London to serve as composer to the Duke of Chandos, for whom he wrote a series of anthems known as the *Chandos Anthems.*

In 1719 a new opera company was formed by a group of peers and businessmen, with Handel as musical director. Handel's operas—he wrote more than thirty in the next thirteen years—scored many successes, but he had a great deal of rivalry and bitterness to put up with, including a free fight on stage between two prima donnas. Eventually the opera company went bankrupt. Handel formed a new company of his own, but ran into further trouble.

Meanwhile Handel had adopted British nationality, anglicising his name from its original form of Georg Friedrich Händel. In between producing operas he wrote a wide variety of music—concertos, anthems, and pieces for special occasions such as royal weddings and George II's coronation. Among the forms with which he experimented were several oratorios. Now, at the height of his misfortunes, he was offered a script for another. It so inspired him that he wrote the music for it in twenty-four days, and gave it the title *Messiah.* It was his masterpiece, but he reserved it for performances in aid of charity. Soon afterwards he abandoned opera finally. From then on it was as a composer of oratorios that he was known and revered. In 1751 his eyesight failed, and he spent his last few years working with the aid of a devoted amenuensis, John Christopher Smith. In spite of his financial troubles he died a rich man, and was given the funeral of a national hero in Westminster Abbey.

Handel's music was strongly influenced by the Italian style, and he combined richness, grandeur, and gaiety in all that he wrote. LUDWIG VAN BEETHOVEN and JOSEPH HAYDN both regarded him as their master, and his music had a lasting influence on that of England, his adopted country.

MAIN COMPOSITIONS 40 operas: including *Rinaldo* (1711), *Rodelina* (1725), *Acis and Galatea* (1732), *Arianna* (1734), *Berenice* (1737), *Serse* (1738); 19 oratorios: *Esther* (1720), *Saul* (1738), *Messiah* (1741), *Semele* (1744), *Judas Maccabaeus* (1746); choral music: anthems, *Te Deums,* odes, cantatas; orchestral: organ concertos, orchestral concertos, *Water Music* (1715), *Music for the Royal Fireworks* (1741); chamber music; harpsichord solos; songs.

# HARRIS, ROY ELLSWORTH (born 1898), was one of the many American composers who studied in Paris with NADIA BOULANGER. In his early years Harris had to treat music as a leisure occupation, earning his living working on a farm or driving a truck. In his twenties he studied in California with ARTHUR BLISS and then won a fellowship that enabled him to go to Paris. After his return to the United States in 1929 he held a succession of university teaching posts.

Harris's vigorous but rugged music echoes his Middle West and truck-driving background, and has been described as 'aggressively American'. Several of his compositions are based on American ideas, such as his symphonic overture *When Johnny Comes Marching Home.* He combines long sweeping melodies with strong rhythmic drive. Most of his symphonies have been neglected by his fellow-countrymen. His output is very considerable, and includes a wide range of works.

MAIN COMPOSITIONS orchestral: 7 symphonies, *Fantasia* for piano and orchestra, overture *When Johnny Comes Marching Home* (1935), *Kentucky Spring* (1949); choral works; chamber music.

# HAYDN, (FRANZ) JOSEPH (1732–1809), an Austrian musical director, formed what is called the Viennese classical

style of music, and developed the symphony towards its modern form. He was one of the first and greatest writers of string quartets. He came of peasant stock: his father was a wheelwright, who played the harp for amusement. Young Haydn developed a beautiful singing voice, and this led to his recruitment for the choir of St Stephen's Cathedral in Vienna. He stayed there until his voice broke at the age of eighteen.

Suddenly, Haydn found himself thrown on his own resources. He eked out a precarious living playing and teaching until he secured an appointment as *Kapellmeister* to Count Maximilian von Morzin. He stayed there only two years. Then by good fortune he was engaged as assistant *Kapellmeister* by Prince Anton Esterházy, a very wealthy nobleman, and spent most of the rest of his life on the Esterházy estate at Eisenstadt, 48km (30 miles) from Vienna, or at another vast castle, Esterháza. Haydn found himself in charge of a brilliant orchestra, a choir, and later an opera company. Under Prince Anton's brother and successor, Prince Nicolaus, Haydn was encouraged to develop his extraordinary talents as a composer.

It was during one of his visits to Vienna that Haydn met the young WOLFGANG AMADEUS MOZART, and the two men became fast friends. Each learned a great deal from the other —Mozart technique, and Haydn emotional profundity. Gradually his life of isolation began to irk Haydn; but in 1790 Nicolaus died, and his successor, no musician, disbanded the court orchestra, retaining Haydn as *Kapellmeister* but with no duties to perform. For the first time in his life, he was free. He at once settled in Vienna, but his fame, despite his seclusion, was international, and almost at once he was invited to London. There he spent two years, admired and fêted, and wrote some of his finest symphonies. When he returned to Vienna he met the young LUDWIG VAN BEETHOVEN, to whom he gave some lessons, but soon he was back in London for a second visit. At this time he wrote his last and greatest symphonies.

In 1795 Haydn returned to Vienna for good. He wrote a series of Masses for the latest Esterházy prince, Nicolaus II, some string quartets, and two oratorios, *The Seasons* and *The Creation*. He spent his remaining years in semi-retirement, but such was his fame that when the French captured Vienna in 1809 they placed a special guard on his house to protect him.

Haydn's music is distinguished by its freshness and vitality. His earlier works are comparatively simple and straightforward, but in his later period, after he had come under Mozart's influence, he achieved a greater grandeur, depth of thought, and force that prepared the way for the revolution in music that was to be brought about by Beethoven. It is significant that when Austria wanted a new national anthem comparable to Britain's 'God Save the King', the Imperial authorities commissioned Haydn to write it as the one composer who could do so.

Haydn's younger brother Michael (1737–1806) was also a composer, and many of his works have been wrongly attributed to Joseph. Michael was musical director to the Archbishop of Salzburg for much of his life. His later years were marred by an addiction to drink.

MAIN COMPOSITIONS 20 operas, 5 puppet operas; orchestral: 107 symphonies, 50 divertimenti, concertos for organ, harpsichord, violin, cello, horn and other instruments, marches, overtures; 8 oratorios, including *The Creation* (1798), *The Seasons* (1801); other choral music: Masses, *Te Deums*, cantatas, motets; chamber music: 84 string quartets, 56 string trios, 31 piano trios; keyboard music; songs.

HENZE, HANS WERNER (born 1926), a German pianist and conductor, combined the twelve-tone system of music with other, more traditional elements, including on occasion jazz. Henze's musical studies were interrupted by World War II; he served in the German army, and was captured by the British. After the war he spent two years as musical director of the municipal theatre at Constance, then turned his attention fully to composing, experimenting with the twelve-tone system and combining it with other styles. The operatic melodrama *Das Wundertheater* included jazz idioms, and caused somewhat of a sensation. So did his first major opera, *Boulevard Solitude*, which combined not only twelve-tone music and jazz but even arias reminiscent of GIACOMO PUCCINI.

When he was twenty-six Henze decided to leave Germany, feeling out of sympathy with the mood of the country, and settle in Italy, where he remained. During the next twenty years he produced a succession of operas and ballets, which were warmly received by audiences everywhere. He also wrote a great deal of orchestral music, including five symphonies. The rest of his time was taken up with teaching, and in 1961 he became a professor of composition at Salzburg, while continuing to make Italy his home.

MAIN COMPOSITIONS operas: *Das Wundertheater* (1949), *Boulevard Solitude* (1952), *König Hirsch* (1956), *Der Prinz von Homburg* (1960), *Elegie für Junge Liebende* (1961), *Der Junge Lord* (1965), *Die Bassariden* (1966); 9 ballets including *Jack Pudding* (1951), *Anrufung Apolls* (1951), *Undine* (1958); orchestral: 5 symphonies, concertos for piano, violin, oboe, harp, double bass; choral music; piano solos; songs.

HINDEMITH, PAUL (1895–1963), a German viola player, became an international soloist and chamber music player. His career in Germany was cut short by the Nazis, who objected to his association with Jewish musicians. At the age of forty-three Hindemith was forced to leave his country, and after a brief stay in Switzerland he settled in the United States. In 1953 he returned to Switzerland, and he died in his native Germany.

Hindemith's music combines the bold harmonies of the twentieth century with the forms and techniques of the eighteenth. He wrote fugues and passacaglias, and was fond of contrapuntal devices. His experience of the practical side of music-making led him, like his eighteenth-century predecessors, to write music for practical use as well as for its own sake. He coined the term *Gebrauchsmusik* (music for use), though he later disowned it, and also *Hausmusik* (house music), which was aimed at amateurs. His often biting humour is shown by some of his operas, such as *Neues vom Tage* (*News of the Day*) in which the heroine sings an aria in praise of electric heating. *Mathis der Maler* (*Mathis the Painter*) aroused a storm in Nazi Germany because it showed peasants rebelling against authority, and this led directly to Hindemith's departure from Germany.

MAIN COMPOSITIONS operas: *Cardillac* (1926), *Neues vom Tage* (1929), *Wir Bauen eine Stadt* (children's opera, 1930), *Mathis der Maler* (1938), *Die Harmonie der Welt* (1957), *Der Lange Weinachtsmahl* (1961); ballets; orchestral: 2 symphonies, concertos for piano, violin, viola, cello, clarinet, and other instruments; chamber music; choral music; piano solos: *Ludus Tonalis* (1943); song cycles; film music.

HOLST, GUSTAV THEODORE (1874–1934), a trombone player, teacher, and conductor, was a typically English composer by birth and instinct, though his father was Swedish. His name was originally Gustavus von Holst, but he changed it to a more English form during World War I. After playing the trombone in orchestras he became a teacher, his two most important posts being as music master of St Paul's Girls' School and director of music at Morley College, a working men's college in south London.

Holst spent some years studying Sanskrit, and produced a couple of operas, *Sita* and *Savitri*, with Hindu themes. But like many other British musicians of his generation, he came under the spell of English folk music, and spent some time helping to recover and record this heritage of song before it was lost for ever. In addition he was deeply interested in astrology, and this led to the composition of one of his most popular works, the suite *The Planets*. When he was forty-nine Holst had a bad fall in which he struck the back of his head. This had serious effects on his health, making him more withdrawn, and the music of the last ten years of his life is more austere. Probably his most typical work is the tone poem *Egdon Heath*, inspired by the works of Thomas Hardy.

Holst's father, grandfather, and great-grandfather were all professional musicians, and his daughter Imogen Holst also followed in their footsteps.

MAIN COMPOSITIONS operas: *Sita* (1906), *Savitri* (1908), *The Perfect Fool* (1923), *At the Boar's Head* (1925), *The Tale of the Wandering Scholar* (1929); ballets: *The Golden Goose* (1926), *The Morning of the Year* (1927); orchestral: symphony, overtures, suites (*The Planets*, 1920, *St Paul's Suite*, 1913), concerto for two violins; choral works including *The Hymn of Jesus* (1917); chamber music; piano solos; songs.

HONEGGER, ARTHUR (1892–1955), was a Swiss musician who was born in France and spent his life there, becoming a leading figure in French music and for a time a member of the group known as *Les Six*. Fame came to him with such pictorial compositions as *Pacific 231*, a tone-poem portraying a railway locomotive, and *Rugby*, which illustrated the football game. During World War II he played an active part in the resistance movement in his adopted country while it was in German occupation.

MAIN COMPOSITIONS operas: *Judith* (1926), *Antigone* (1927), *Amphion* (1931), *L'Aiglon* (with JACQUES IBERT, 1937), *Charles le Téméraire* (1944); ballets; choral works: *Le Roi David* (1921), *Jeanne d'Arc* (1938), *La Danse des Morts* (1940); orchestral: 5 symphonies, concertos, descriptive pieces (*Pacific 231*, 1924, *Rugby*, 1928); chamber music, piano solos; songs; film scores.

HUMPERDINCK, ENGELBERT (1854–1921), a German music teacher and critic, is best known for his children's opera *Hänsel und Gretel*. His music captured perfectly the charm and mood of the Grimm brothers' fairy story on which it was based. None of his other operas was so successful.

MAIN COMPOSITIONS operas: *Hänsel und Gretel* (1893), *Die*

*sieben Geislein* (1895), *Dornröschen* (1902), *Die Heirat wider Willen* (1905), *Königskinder* (1910), *Die Marketenderin* (1914), *Gaudeamus* (1919); incidental music; orchestral: *Humoreske, Moorish Rhapsody;* piano works; chamber music; songs.

IBERT, JACQUES FRANÇOIS ANTOINE (1890–1962), a French musical director, is probably best known for the piano solo *Le Petit âne blanc,* from his suite *Histoires.* His studies (under, among others, GABRIEL FAURÉ and NADIA BOULANGER) were interrupted by service in the French navy during World War I. Among the posts he held were those of director of the French academy in Rome and the Paris Opéra. He wrote a variety of works in a variety of styles, and was a master of orchestration.

MAIN COMPOSITIONS operas: *Angélique* (1927), *Persée et Andromède* (1929), *Le Roi d'Yvetot* (1930), *Gonzague* (1935), *L'Aiglon* (with ARTHUR HONNEGER, 1937), *Barbe-Bleu* (radio, 1951); ballets; orchestral: *La Ballade de la geôle de Reading, Escales,* concertos for flute, cello; choral works; chamber music; piano solos; songs; film scores.

IRELAND, JOHN NICHOLSON (1879–1962), an English teacher and pianist, is remembered for his songs, especially 'Sea Fever', a setting of a poem by John Masefield. Ireland wrote mainly for his own instrument, the piano, and he produced a great many witty and delicate pieces for it. Of his orchestral works the impressionistic pieces *Mai-Dun* and *The Forgotten Rite* are the most typical.

MAIN COMPOSITIONS orchestral: tone poems *The Forgotten Rite* (1913), *Mai-Dun* (1921), *London Overture* (1936), *Concertino Pastorale* (1939); choral works: *These Things Shall Be* (1937); Church music; chamber music; piano solos; organ solos; songs.

IVES, CHARLES EDWARD (1874–1954), a United States businessman, was one of the most original of American composers. The son of a bandmaster, he studied music at Yale University, then deliberately chose the insurance world as a career because, as he said, 'how can a composer let his wife and children starve on his dissonances?' Ives's music is difficult to perform and to listen to. His fourth symphony, performed for the first time eleven years after his death, and nearly fifty years after its composition, contains in one section twenty-seven rhythms at once. His second symphony, completed in 1902, had to wait a similar time for a first performance. His third, written in 1911, won him the Pulitzer Prize in 1947. For his last twenty-four years Ives lived as a recluse on a farm in Connecticut, never even reading the newspapers.

Much of Ives's music is programme music, closely connected in thought to the people of America, and bearing such titles as *Three Places in New England* and *Fourth of July*.

MAIN COMPOSITIONS orchestral: 4 symphonies, many 'programme' pieces; chamber music; choral music; 114 songs.

JANÁČEK, LEOŠ (1854–1928), an organist, conductor, and teacher, was a Czech musician who evolved a style based partly on folk music. When he was born his country formed part of Austria–Hungary, an unwieldy empire sprawling over central Europe. Janáček's studies took him to Vienna, the Austrian capital, and also to Germany and Russia, but he returned to his homeland to found an organ college at Brno in Moravia, the central part of modern Czechoslovakia. After Czechoslovakia attained independence, Janáček became a professor at the Prague conservatory.

MAIN COMPOSITIONS 10 operas including *Jeji pastorkyňa* (*Jenůfa*, 1904), *Vylet Pana Broucka* (1920), *Káťa Kabanová* (1921), *Příhody Lišky Bystroušky* (1924), *Vec Makropulos* (1926), *Z Mrtvého domu* (1930); orchestral works; chamber music; sacred music including a *Glagolitic Mass* (a traditional Slav Mass); songs.

JANNEQUIN, CLÉMENT (*c.* 1473–*c.* 1560), an early French composer, wrote *chansons* for many voices and was one of

65

E

the first writers of 'programme music'. Many of his pieces bear fanciful titles suggestive of their character, such as *The Song of the Birds*, *The Battle of Marignan*, and *The Cries of Paris*. Little is known of his life, but it is thought that he was a priest and a pupil of JOSQUIN DES PRÉS, and that he lived in Bordeaux and Anjou—and possibly Rome—before settling in Paris. He was in the service of the French king Henri II in the last years of his life.

MAIN COMPOSITIONS 2 Masses; motets; 286 chansons; other vocal works.

JOSQUIN DES PRÉS (*c.* 1440–1521), a Flemish musician, was the leading member of the Netherlands school of composers who dominated Europe at the start of the sixteenth century. He was born probably at Condé-sur-L'Escaut, now in northern France. He went to Italy, as did many Flemish musicians at that time. Later he was for a while in the service of the Holy Roman Emperor Maximilian I. He became a priest and spent his last years back in Condé-sur-L'Escaut.

Josquin played a large part in music's transition from the medieval tradition to the freer counterpoint of the Renaissance. He had many pupils, including CLÉMENT JANNEQUIN.

MAIN COMPOSITIONS 20 Masses; 150 motets; 50 songs.

KHACHATURIAN, ARAM ILYICH (born 1903), a Russian-Armenian cellist, became famous for one piece—the Sabre Dance from his ballet *Gayaneh*. He was the first Armenian composer to achieve world-wide renown for his music. His work was along strictly orthodox Soviet lines, which won him four Stalin Prizes and a Lenin Prize.

MAIN COMPOSITIONS ballets: *Happiness* (1929), *Gayaneh* (1942), *Spartacus* (1953); orchestral: symphonies, concertos for piano, cello, violin; chamber music; film music.

KODÁLY, ZOLTÁN (1882–1967), a Hungarian music teacher, was closely associated with BÉLA BARTÓK in the collection of Hungarian folk music, on which he became an authority. His best known work is probably the comic opera *Háry János*, from which he compiled an orchestral suite that remains a concert-hall favourite. At the age of twenty-five he was appointed professor of theory and composition at the Budapest conservatory, where he stayed for thirty-five years.

MAIN COMPOSITIONS operas: *Háry János* (1926), *Czinka Panna* (1948); orchestral: symphony, Hungarian dance suites, concerto for orchestra; choral: *Psalmus Hungaricus* (1923), *Te Deum* (1936), *Missa Brevis* (1944); folk song collections.

KREISLER, FRITZ (1875–1962), an Austrian-born violinist, won world-wide fame for the beauty of his tone and his smooth cantabile style of playing. Besides performing most of the master works in the violinist's repertory, he also delighted audiences with a number of short pieces which he published as arrangements of works by eighteenth-century composers. In 1935 he caused a sensation by admitting that the 'arrangements' were in fact original compositions of his own in the style of various classical writers.

Kreisler made his debut as a player while still a boy, then abandoned his musical career for a time to study medicine, and to do a period of compulsory military service as an officer in the Austrian army. He took up his career as a violinist again in 1898. It was interrupted for a very short while by service in the trenches during World War I, but in 1915 he settled in the United States, which was his home for the rest of his life. He became a US citizen in 1943.

MAIN COMPOSITIONS operettas: *Appleblossom* (1919), *The Marriage Knot* (1923); original works and transcriptions for violin and piano and other instruments; chamber music; songs.

LALO, VICTOR ANTOINE ÉDOUARD (1823–92), a French violinist and violist of Spanish descent, is remembered for his chamber music, and especially for his *Symphonie Espagnole*, a rhapsodic violin concerto, brilliant and full of Spanish flavour. He also succeeded strikingly in his works for orchestra and the stage, particularly the opera *Le Roi d'Ys*.

MAIN COMPOSITIONS operas: *Fiesque* (1866), *Le Roi d'Ys* (1888); ballets *Namouna* (1882), *Nerou* (1891); orchestral: symphonies, *Norwegian Rhapsody*, *Symphonie Espagnole*, violin, cello, and piano concertos; Church music; chamber music; songs.

LASSO, ORLANDO DI (*c.* 1532–94), was one of the greatest of the many Flemish composers whose music dominated Europe in the fifteenth and sixteenth centuries. His name was probably Orlande Lassus, but he often used the Italian form of it. As a boy he had a beautiful voice, and at about the age of twelve he entered the service of Ferdinand of Gonzaga, an Italian prince, who took him to Italy. Some time after his voice broke he was appointed *maestro di cappella* to the church of St John Lateran. Soon afterwards he returned home to see his parents, only to find them both dead. For a time he settled in Antwerp. Then Duke Albert V of Bavaria offered him a post in his chapel at Munich; there Lasso stayed for the rest of his life, becoming *Kapellmeister* in his early thirties. He visited Italy where he received a knighthood from the Pope. Duke Albert raised him to the nobility, and he married the daughter of a lady of the court. His letters show him to have been full of fun and wit, though in his later years he suffered from melancholy spells.

Lasso was equally at home setting the words of the Latin Mass or those of bawdy drinking songs and delicate love songs in French, German, and Italian. His settings are distinguished both by the appropriateness of the music to the words, and by a willingness to experiment.

MAIN COMPOSITIONS 41 Masses; 100 *Magnificats*; 100 motets; 200 madrigals; many chansons, villanellas, morescas, and part-songs.

LEHÁR, FRANZ (1870–1948), a Hungarian bandmaster, won world fame with his light operas. He became a bandmaster at the age of twenty. Six years later his first operetta, *Kukuscha*, was produced at Leipzig. When he was thirty-five *The Merry Widow* brought him instant success and fortune, with its gay tunes and brilliant orchestration.

MAIN COMPOSITIONS grand opera *Giuditta* (1934); operettas, including *Kukuscha* (1896), *The Merry Widow* (1905), *The Count of Luxembourg* (1909), *Gipsy Love* (1910), *The Man With Three Wives* (1908), *Frasquita* (1922), *Paganini* (1925), *Frederica* (1928), *The Land of Smiles* (1923); orchestral: violin concerto, dances, marches; piano solos.

LEONCAVALLO, RUGGIERO (1858–1919), an Italian musician who began his career as a café pianist, is remembered for one two-act opera, *I Pagliacci*. Leoncavallo studied at the Naples conservatory, and earned his living as an itinerant pianist and teacher while he composed. His first two works met with no success, but *I Pagliacci,* produced in Milan when he was thirty-four, was a triumph. His later works brought him little further renown. Leoncavallo based the story of *I Pagliacci* (*The Clowns*) on a real-life murder; at the trial his own father had been the judge.

MAIN COMPOSITIONS operas: *Chatterton* (1896), *I Pagliacci* (1892), *I Medici* (1893), *La Bohème* (1897), *Zazà* (1900), *Der Roland von Berlin* (1904), *Edipo Re* (1920).

LISZT, FRANZ (1811–86), a Hungarian pianist, was one of the dominant figures in European music during the mid-1800s, and a deft and original composer. His father was a steward in the service of the Esterházy family (for whom JOSEPH HAYDN worked for so long). Liszt was a brilliant prodigy, and several noblemen subscribed to a fund to have him trained. By the time he was thirteen, Liszt had an international reputation as a pianist, and had had his first (and last) opera produced with success. At the age of seventeen he decided he wanted to become a priest, and for a time he gave up public playing.

Liszt returned to active music after hearing NICCOLÒ

PAGANINI, whose playing fired him with enthusiasm. When he was twenty-two he fell in love with a married woman, the twenty-eight-year-old Countess Marie d'Agoult, and lived with her for four years in Switzerland and Italy. They had three children. Meanwhile Liszt had regained his reputation as one of the greatest pianists of the day. In 1839 he parted from the countess and embarked on eight years of concert tours, during which he was fêted and lionised—and had many love affairs.

In 1847 Liszt gave up his career as a concert pianist and settled down at Weimar, where he already held the post of director of music. He also acquired a new mistress, the Princess Carolyne von Sayn-Wittgenstein, who was separated from her husband. She was an eccentric person, who smoked cigars and preferred to stay awake at night and sleep by day. During his Weimar period Liszt composed a great deal, and was always ready to help other musicians, among them RICHARD WAGNER. Eventually the intrigues of others made Liszt's position at Weimar impossible, and he resigned. Soon after, Carolyne went to Rome to petition the Pope for a divorce, so that she and Liszt could marry. It was granted, but at the last moment the Pope refused to permit Liszt to marry her.

For the next eight years Liszt and his princess lived in Rome, but not together. For this, Carolyne's habit of avoiding both daylight and fresh air may have been responsible. Liszt had returned to his religious interests, and in 1865 he received minor orders. Henceforth he was known as the Abbé Liszt. About this time his daughter Cosima left her husband, the pianist Hans von Bülow, and went off to live with Wagner, whom she eventually married. Strangely, considering Liszt's own life, this led to a coolness between himself and Wagner.

Liszt's music is very varied. Some of it is superficial and showy, designed to display his extraordinary technique as a pianist. During his later years he wrote a great deal in which he explored new ideas of tonality—ideas which led in due course to the atonal music of ARNOLD SCHÖNBERG. But perhaps his greatest contribution to music was in popularising that of others, including BEETHOVEN and Wagner, and encouraging the younger musicians of his day.

MAIN COMPOSITIONS opera *Don Sanche* (1825); orchestral: 2 symphonies, 2 piano concertos, 12 symphonic poems; choral: *The Legend of St Elizabeth* (1862), *Psalm XIII* (1863), *Christus* (1866); piano solos; piano transcriptions; organ solos; songs.

LULLY, JEAN-BAPTISTE (1632–87), an Italian-born French violinist, revolutionised opera in his adopted country. He was taken to France as a boy, probably as a servant of the Duc de Guise, and by the time he was twenty was a violinist in the string band of Louis XIV. Soon he had added the duties of court-composer, and began writing ballet music and incidental music for the plays of Molière. As unscrupulous as he was talented, Lully used every device of court intrigue to rise in his profession, and by the time he was thirty had absolute control of the music of the court. Ten years later he had made a fortune, and was able to buy from the dramatist Abbé Perrin his monopoly of opera in France.

Lully made ruthless use of his monopoly to put all his rivals out of business, and began to write operas. His first productions were a great success, and in the next fourteen years he produced about twenty more. The style he set for opera involved abandoning the *recitativo secco*—a sort of half spoken, half sung narration to the barest harpsichord accompaniment—in favour of a sung recitative with a fuller accompaniment, which blended more closely with the arias.

Lully lived in a court which was a hotbed of vice and intrigue, and he took a large part in both. The king was broadminded, to put it mildly, but even he disapproved of some of Lully's excesses and only the genius of the composer, coupled with his clowning and acting which kept the king in fits of laughter, saved him from serious trouble. With all his scandalous behaviour, it is ironic that Lully should

71

have died from an abscess on the foot, caused by striking it with his long baton while conducting a *Te Deum.*

MAIN COMPOSITIONS operas including *Cadmus et Hermione* (1673), *Alceste* (1674), *Thésée* (1675), *Atys* (1676), *Isis* (1677), *Psyche* (1678), *Bellérophon* (1679), *Proserpine* (1680), *Persée* (1682), *Phaéton* (1683), *Amadis de Gaule* (1684), *Roland* (1685), *Armide et Renaud* (1686), *Acis et Galathée* (1686); ballets; incidental music for the stage; sacred works, including *Te Deum* and motets; dances; instrumental suites.

MACHAUT, GUILLAUME DE (*c.* 1300–77), a French priest and poet, played an important part in the development of music in France, both in harmony and in his mastery of polyphonic writing. Machaut became chaplain and secretary to King John of Bohemia, and later settled at Rheims, where he was made a canon. He had a great reputation as a romantic poet, and set many of his own *lais, ballades,* and *rondeaux* to music.

MAIN COMPOSITIONS Church music: *Mass for Four Voices,* 23 motets; other vocal works: 42 ballades, 19 lais, 21 rondeaux, 33 virelais.

MAHLER, GUSTAV (1860–1911), an Austrian Jewish conductor and teacher, is known principally for his songs and his symphonies. He wished to devote his time to composition, but had to take a series of posts as a theatre and opera conductor to earn his living. Unfortunately his bluntness and lack of tact made his fellow musicians dislike him.

Mahler's music, inspired by that of LUDWIG VAN BEETHOVEN and ANTON BRUCKNER, tends to be on the grand scale. Indeed, his eighth symphony is known as *The Symphony of a Thousand* from the enormous forces required for it—850 in the chorus, eight soloists, and an orchestra of 146. The song cycle *Das Lied von der Erde,* settings of Chinese poems, is also a choral symphony in all but name.

MAIN COMPOSITIONS operas: *Die Argonauten, Herzog*

*Ernst von Schwaben*; orchestral: 9 symphonies (a 10th was completed by Deryck Cooke), *Das Lied von der Erde*; songs.

MARTINŮ, BOHUSLAV (1890–1959), a Czech composer, produced a prodigious quantity of music in the course of a life that was often difficult. He studied first in Prague and then in Paris. There he was closely linked to the group known as *Les Six*, which included ARTHUR HONNEGER, DARIUS MILHAUD, and FRANCIS POULENC. He remained in Paris until June 1940, when he and his wife fled before the advancing Germans, leaving many manuscripts and personal possessions. They emigrated to the United States, returning to Prague for the last few years of Martinů's life. His work is often reminiscent of the nineteenth century, but with busy and dominating rhythms and some powerful discords.

MAIN COMPOSITIONS operas; ballet; orchestral: 6 symphonies, concertos and other works for piano, violin, cello, harpsichord; chamber music; piano solos; choral music; songs; film music.

MASCAGNI, PIETRO (1863–1945), an Italian conductor and piano teacher, is remembered for one composition—the ever popular one-act opera *Cavalleria Rusticana*. It won him first prize in a competition when he was twenty-six, and has remained in operatic repertoires ever since, usually performed as a companion piece to RUGGIERO LEONCAVALLO'S two-act *I Pagliacci*. His later works had little success.

MAIN COMPOSITIONS operas: *Cavalleria Rusticana* (1890), *L'Amico Fritz* (1891), *Iris* (1898), *Le Maschere* (1901), *Isabeau* (1911), *Il Piccolo Marat* (1921), *Nerone* (1935); choral works, including a *Requiem*; orchestral works, including a symphony; film scores.

MASSENET, JULES ÉMILE FRÉDÉRIC (1842–1912), a French teacher of the piano and composition, wrote twenty-seven operas which enjoyed considerable success in his lifetime. But he is remembered chiefly for his masterpiece

*Manon,* written when he was in his early forties. His earlier works are his best; in his later operas he tended to repeat himself in a series of musical clichés. After studying at the Paris conservatory and winning the Prix de Rome he spent some time as a tympanist in a theatre orchestra.

MAIN COMPOSITIONS operas: *La Grand'tante* (1867), *Don César de Bazan* (1872), *Eve* (1875), *Le Roi de Lahore* (1877), *Hérodiade* (1881), *Manon* (1884), *Werther* (1892), *Thaïs* (1894), *La Navarraise* (1894), *Le Jongleur de Notre-Dame* (1902), *Chérubin* (1905), *Ariane* (1906), *Thérèse* (1907), *Bacchus* (1909), *Don Quichotte* (1910), *Roma* (1912), *Panurge* (1913), *Cléopâtre* (1914), *Amadis* (1922); ballets; orchestral works, including piano concertos; choral works; songs.

## MENDELSSOHN-BARTHOLDY, (JACOB LUDWIG) FELIX (1809–47), generally known as *Felix Mendelssohn,* came of a well-to-do German Jewish family who took the additional name Bartholdy on adopting the Christian faith. Felix's grandfather, Moses Mendelssohn, was a leading philosopher of the eighteenth century. Mendelssohn's genius appeared early, and he was given every encouragement to develop as a pianist and composer. One of his earliest compositions was the overture to Shakespeare's *A Midsummer Night's Dream,* which he wrote when he was seventeen. He was passionately fond of the works of JOHANN SEBASTIAN BACH, and when he was only twenty revived Bach's *St Matthew Passion*—its first performance since Bach's death. This led directly to the great revival of interest in Bach's work that has lasted to the present day.

Soon afterwards he began to travel, as pianist, conductor and composer. He paid several visits to England, where he became Queen Victoria's favourite musician, and to Scotland, where he was inspired to write the overture *Fingal's Cave.* There were so many calls on his time that he was constantly travelling and over-working, which hastened his early death.

Something of Mendelssohn's feverish, energetic nature

shows in his music, but generally he combines the lushness of the Romantic movement with the precision and regularity of the Classical style that preceded it. Perhaps his best-loved work is his violin concerto in E minor over which he took endless pains; it remains one of the most expressive compositions ever written for the instrument. The same lyrical spirit is found in his *Songs Without Words* for piano solo.

MAIN COMPOSITIONS 3 operas (one unfinished); orchestral: 5 symphonies, 7 overtures, 2 piano concertos, 2 violin concertos; oratorios: *St Paul* (1836), *Elijah* (1846); incidental music to *A Midsummer Night's Dream;* chamber music; piano solos: *Songs Without Words*; songs.

MENOTTI, GIAN-CARLO (born 1911), an Italian-born musician who made his home and his career in the United States, became famous as a composer of light operas, though many of them have a serious vein. He wrote his first opera at the age of eleven. Typical of his works is *The Telephone,* a one-act frolic. Much of his work was designed for television or radio. He founded the Festival of Two Worlds at Spoleto, in Italy, to help young musicians. He wrote all his own libretti, most of them in English.

MAIN COMPOSITIONS operas: *Amelia Goes to the Ball* (1936), *The Old Maid and the Thief* (radio, 1939), *The Medium* (1946), *The Telephone* (1947), *Amahl and the Night Visitors* (TV, 1949), *The Consul* (1950, Pulitzer Prize), *The Saint of Bleeker Street* (1954, Pulitzer Prize), *Maria Golovin* (TV, 1957), *The Unicorn, the Gorgon, and the Manticore* (1957), *The Last Savage* (1963), *Martin's Lie* (1964); ballet *Sebastian* (1944); orchestral works including piano and violin concertos; oratorio *The Death of the Bishop of Brindisi* (1963).

MESSIAEN, OLIVIER EUGÈNE PROSPER CHARLES (born 1908), a French organist and teacher, became as important for his influence on other composers as for his own often highly mystical works. He was one of the founders of a group of composers called *La Jeune France*. In World War II he fought in the army and was a prisoner of war for a time, returning to become a professor at the Paris conservatory. He was a tireless experimenter in rhythms, and embodied his highly individual theories in long treatises.

MAIN COMPOSITIONS orchestral including *Trois petites liturgies de la présence divine* (1944), symphony *Turangalîla* (1948), *Chronochromie* (1960); choral including a Mass (1933); organ solos; imitations of birdsong. TREATISES *Technique de mon langage musical* (1944), *Quatre études de rhythme* (1950).

MEYERBEER, GIACOMO (1791–1864), was a German-Jewish composer and pianist who became a leading influence on French opera. He was originally named *Jakob Liebmann Beer,* and he was born into a wealthy business family. Money and his own great musical skill gained him first-class teachers. His early works having had no success in Germany, he went to Italy at the age of twenty-five. There he wrote a number of successful operas in the Italian style, influenced by the music of GIOACCHINO ROSSINI. At the age of thirty-nine he moved to Paris, where he produced the opera *Robert le Diable,* which was an enormous success. For some years his music dominated Paris; later he was appointed *Generalmusikdirektor* in Berlin, and divided his time between the two cities. He helped RICHARD WAGNER to get his *Flying Dutchman* performed, and Wagner repaid him by flattery to his face, and anonymous articles reviling his music (he called him 'a Jew banker who writes music').

MAIN COMPOSITIONS operas: *Jephthas Gelübde* (1812), *Wirt und Gast* (1813), *Romilda e Costanza* (1817), *Semiramide Riconosciuta* (1819), *Emma di Resburgo* (1819), *Margherita d'Anjou* (1820), *L'Esule di Granata* (1822), *Il Crociato in Egitto* (1824), *Robert le Diable* (1831), *Les Huguenots* (1836), *Ein Feldlager in Schlesien* (1844), *Le Prophète* (1849), *L'Étoile du Nord* (1854), *Dinorah* (1859),

*L'Africaine* (1865); oratorio: *Gott und die Natur* (1811); instrumental music; vocal music including cantatas; songs.

MILHAUD, DARIUS (born 1892), a French composer, was one of the group of composers known as *Les Six* (others included ARTHUR HONNEGER and FRANCIS POULENC). He developed strongly the technique of polytonality, in which the music can be in several keys at once (as many as six in his third symphony). A prolific composer, Milhaud wrote a very wide variety of music. After studying with PAUL DUKAS and VINCENT D'INDY he spent two years in the diplomatic service in Brazil, and from the age of thirty spent much of his time in the United States, where he came under the influence of jazz. In association with the writers Jean Cocteau and Paul Claudel he produced a number of ballets, of which *Le Boeuf sur le toit* is the most famous.

MAIN COMPOSITIONS operas: *Le Pauvre Matelot* (1926); *Christophe Colomb* (1930), *Bolivar* (1943), *David* (1954); ballets: *L'Homme et son désir, La Création du Monde, Le Boeuf sur le toit*; orchestral, including symphonies; chamber music; choral works; film and radio music.

MONTEVERDI, CLAUDIO (1567–1643), was the first major composer of operas. He was the son of a doctor at Cremona, the little north Italian town where so many famous violin-makers worked. He studied in Cremona with the local *maestro di cappella,* and made such progress that at the age of about twenty-four he secured a post as viol player at the court of Vincenzo Gonzaga, Duke of Mantua. After ten years' service he was promoted to be *maestro della musica* at Mantua. During this period he composed and published a number of madrigals and other vocal works.

In 1607 Monteverdi's first opera, *La Favola d'Orfeo*, was performed, just ten years after the first true opera, Jacopo Peri's *Dafne*. Its instant success showed how well Monteverdi had grasped the possibilities of this new art form. In the same year his wife, Claudia, died, but Monteverdi had no time for mourning, as the Duke ordered him to write another opera to celebrate his heir's wedding the following year. This was *L'Arianna*, most of the music of which is lost. A few years later the Duke of Mantua died and his son dismissed Monteverdi.

Monteverdi's pay had been small and the work hard, and he left Mantua with virtually no money. After a year's rest, spent partly at his father's home, he was suddenly appointed *maestro di cappella* at St Mark's Cathedral, Venice, where he remained for the rest of his life. At the age of sixty-five he was ordained a priest, following the example of his elder son Francesco. During his thirty years at Venice, Monteverdi continued to write madrigals and sacred choral works, and also composed a number of operas, most of which are lost. His last work, *L'Incoronazione di Poppea*, was written at the age of seventy-five. It is his masterpiece among the surviving works, though the morals of the story, in which the wicked triumph, make it an odd choice for an elderly priest.

Monteverdi's music is marked by his mastery of writing for the voice, and by his great range of emotions from tragedy to comedy. His writing for the opera orchestra, the size and form of which he helped to evolve, shows his grasp of the instrumentation of his day.

MAIN COMPOSITIONS operas: *La Favola d'Orfeo* (1607), *L'Arianna* (1608), *Il Combattimento di Tancredi e Clorinda* (1624), *Il Ritorno d'Ulisse in Patria* (1641), *L'Incoronazione di Poppea* (1642); ballets; Church music: Masses, *Vespro della Beata Virgine* (1610); madrigals; canzonets; *Scherzi Musicali*.

MORLEY, THOMAS (*c*. 1557–*c*. 1603), an organist and court musician, was the first great English writer of madrigals. His *A Plaine and Easie Introduction to Practicall Musicke* was one of the most important textbooks of its day, and is still an invaluable guide to music of the sixteenth century. He held various organ appointments, including one at St Paul's Cathedral, London. In 1591 he was engaged in some form of anti-Roman Catholic espionage in the Netherlands, presumably on behalf of the English Crown. The following year he became a Gentleman of the Chapel Royal, a court appointment, which he held until shortly before his death. One of Morley's London neighbours was William Shakespeare, and Morley's best known song is 'It was a Lover and His Lass', from Shakespeare's *As You Like It.*

Morley's earlier music is in the English tradition of good solid counterpoint, but in his later works he adopted the Italian madrigal style. Towards the end of his life he edited a collection of 29 madrigals in honour of Queen Elizabeth I, entitled *The Triumphs of Oriana,* to which he contributed two madrigals. Although each of the 29 ends with the words 'Long live fair Oriana', publication was so delayed that despite the date of 1601 on the title page it did not appear until 1603 when Elizabeth was already dead.

MAIN COMPOSITIONS *Canzonets for Three Voices* (1593), *Madrigals for Four Voices* (1594), *Ballets for Five Voices and Canzonets for Two Voices* (1595), *Book of Consort Lessons* (1599), *Airs to Sing and Play to the Lute with Bass Viol* (1600); settings of Church services; motets; anthems. BOOK *A Plaine and Easie Introduction to Practicall Musicke* (1597).

MOZART, WOLFGANG AMADEUS (1756–91), was one of the most gifted musicians the world has ever seen. He was a brilliant virtuoso pianist; his father once told him that if he chose he could be the finest violinist of his day; and he produced some of the most perfectly written music ever composed. His father, Leopold Mozart, was a violinist and composer in the service of the Archbishop of Salzburg, in Austria. Wolfgang was christened *Johannes Chrysostomus Wolfgangus Theophilus.* He never used the first two names, and adopted the French form of the last name, Amadé. People ever since have used the Latin form, Amadeus. It means 'love of God'.

Mozart was a precocious child, an accomplished harpsi-

79

chord player by the time he was six and already composing little pieces. His father decided to take young Wolfgang and his sister Maria Anna, called 'Nannerl', on tour as prodigies, hoping to make a fortune and provide for their futures. He began a series of tours two weeks before Mozart's sixth birthday, going first to Munich and then to Vienna. A year later Leopold and the two children set off on a grand tour, visiting Paris, London—where they stayed sixteen months—and The Hague. The tour lasted over three years. In London Mozart had lessons from JOHANN CHRISTIAN BACH, whose music influenced him greatly. During the next few years Leopold took his son three times to Italy and twice to Vienna. Between and during these tours the boy was kept hard at his musical studies.

All his life Mozart loved opera, and his first, *La Finta Semplice,* was written and produced when he was thirteen. Soon commissions for others followed, while in between Mozart dashed off a stream of compositions including symphonies and Church music. At the age of sixteen the Archbishop of Salzburg gave him a post as *Konzertmeister,* but a limit was put on his travels. As a servant of the archbishop, Mozart was expected to remain at his post. When he was twenty-two he obtained his discharge and set off to seek his fortune elsewhere. Leopold was unable to accompany him, but his mother went with him to keep an eye on him. They went to Paris, where disaster struck; Mozart was unable to find a post, and his mother died. Sadly, Mozart returned to Salzburg, and a position as court organist. It was a position of drudgery.

A year later, the Elector of Bavaria borrowed Mozart to write an opera for him. The work, *Idomeneo,* was a resounding success, but in the midst of his triumph the archbishop summoned Mozart to join him in Vienna, forbade him to play for anyone else, and forced him to eat with the servants —Mozart ranked below the archbishop's valets but above his cooks. After an angry scene, Mozart asked for his freedom. He got it, together with a kick on the behind from the archbishop's steward. Mozart settled down in Vienna, and soon afterwards married Constanze Weber, a cousin of CARL MARIA VON WEBER.

From then on Mozart led a precarious life, teaching, playing the piano, composing operas, piano concertos and other music, but seldom earning much money. For relaxation he played billiards and skittles, and often found inspiration while engaged in a game. He had several enemies, jealous of his talents, but many friends. The most important of these friends was JOSEPH HAYDN. The two composers learned a great deal from each other. They often used to play string quartets, Haydn leading, Mozart playing the viola, and the other parts taken by two other well-known composers of their day, Karl Ditters von Dittersdorf and Johann Vanhall.

Mozart took endless trouble with the many operas he composed during his last years in Vienna, tailoring each part to suit the soloist engaged for the performance. He won fame throughout Europe, but his debts grew, and he could not obtain a well-paid, settled post. Worried and overworked, Mozart became ill. In 1791, he received a commission for a Requiem Mass, and became convinced that he would be writing it for himself. Before he could complete it he was asked to write an opera at short notice for the Holy Roman Emperor Leopold II. Mozart wrote the opera and travelled to Prague to rehearse and conduct it in just eighteen days. Then he returned to Vienna, where he died from rheumatic fever, with the Requiem still unfinished. It was completed by his pupil, Franz Süssmayer.

Mozart's music appears elegant because of the perfection and polish that he bestowed on it. But it is much more profound than it seems, full of wit, humour, and on occasion grief. Every note is important, and for this reason many musicians find it among the most taxing to play.

Pieces by Mozart are generally referred to by their numbers in a catalogue compiled in the mid-1800s by the musician Ludwig von Köchel; these numbers are known as Köchel numbers, Köchel usually being abbreviated to K.

MAIN COMPOSITIONS operas: *La Finta Semplice* (1769), *Idomeneo* (1781), *Die Entführung aus dem Serail* (1782), *Le Nozze di Figaro* (1786), *Don Giovanni* (1787), *Così fan Tutte* (1790), *Die Zauberflöte* (1791), *La Clemenza di Tito* (1791); orchestral: nearly 50 symphonies, divertimentos, serenades, concertos for piano, violin, horn, bassoon, flute, oboe, clarinet; Church music; chamber music; piano solos; songs.

MUSGRAVE, THEA (born 1928), became one of the few women composers to achieve a world-wide reputation, both for her music and as a teacher. She was born in Edinburgh, where she studied, but later spent most of her time in London or travelling. In her work she combines a masterly technique of conventional composition with a readiness to experiment with such modern devices as electronic music and the use of 'chance' and mobility of instruments. In *Memento Vitae,* a concerto which is dedicated to LUDWIG VAN BEETHOVEN, she uses quotations from Beethoven's own works. She is particularly fond of the concerto, both for solo instruments and as an orchestral work.

MAIN COMPOSITIONS operas: *The Abbot of Drimock* (1955), *The Decision* (1965); ballet: *Beauty and the Beast* (1968); orchestral: concertos for orchestra, viola, horn, clarinet, *Memento Vitae* (1969); vocal: *Cantata for a Summer's Day* (1954), *The Phoenix and the Turtle* (1962); chamber music.

MUSSORGSKY, MODESTE PETROVICH (1839–81), a Russian soldier and civil servant, was the most strongly national of the group of Russian composers known as 'The Five' (the others were MILI BALAKIREV, ALEKSANDR BORODIN, César Cui, and NIKOLAI RIMSKY-KORSAKOV). Although Mussorgsky studied for a while with Balakirev, he remained essentially a gifted amateur. The son of a wealthy landowner, Mussorgsky became an army cadet at the age of thirteen. Five years later he met Cui, also an army officer, and through him other musicians, and decided to make music his career. He left the army the following year. In 1861 new laws liberating serfs destroyed the family wealth and two years later Mussorgsky had to take a job in the civil service. The tragedy of his life was that he developed a fondness for drink, which soon mastered him and possibly contributed to his early death from spinal disease.

In spite of his inability to control his own life and habits, Mussorgsky worked hard to develop and foster a truly Russian style, and he succeeded brilliantly in his masterpiece, the opera *Boris Godunov*.

MAIN COMPOSITIONS operas: *Boris Godunov* (1874), *Khovanschchina* (completed by Rimsky-Korsakov, 1886), *Sorochinsky Fair* (completed by several others, 1913–33); orchestral: *Night on the Bare Mountain* (1872); piano works, including *Pictures at an Exhibition*; songs and song cycles.

NIELSEN, CARL AUGUST (1865–1931), a violinist and conductor, became Denmark's leading composer. After studying the violin he joined the army as a boy bugler, but his talent was spotted by an eminent musician, Niels Gade, who enabled him to study at the Copenhagen conservatory. His career took him from violinist in the court orchestra through various conductorships to be a professor at the conservatory. His music developed from romanticism to polytonality—writing in several keys simultaneously. He also wrote a number of popular songs.

MAIN COMPOSITIONS operas: *Saul og David* (1902), *Maskerade* (1906); orchestral: 6 symphonies, concertos for violin, clarinet, flute; choral works; chamber music; piano solos.

OFFENBACH, JACQUES (1819–80), was a German Jewish cellist, who settled in Paris and became a Roman Catholic and a French citizen. He is famous for his gay operettas, of which he wrote about a hundred, many of them still performed. Offenbach's name at first was *Jacob Wiener*, but his father, a cantor in the synagogue at Cologne, was often called 'Der Offenbacher' because he came from the village of Offenbach, and he adopted the new name. Offenbach was taken to Paris as a boy because the French were more tolerant of Jews than the Germans were. He became a cellist in the orchestra of the Opéra-Comique, and then a conductor at the Théâtre Français. After five years there, despairing of persuading anyone to produce his works, he raised enough money to take over a theatre of his own, which he called the Bouffes-Parisiens. There he scored several small successes. His first real triumph was *Orphée aux Enfers*, a light hearted frolic still frequently revived (in England as *Orpheus in the Underground*).

Offenbach became a French citizen in 1860. When war between the French and the Germans broke out in 1870 he felt himself in an awkward position, and retired to Italy until peace was restored. He returned to Paris to a life of hard work culminating in a serious opera, *The Tales of Hoffmann*. He hoped this would live on when his lighter works were forgotten, and it is generally accepted as his masterpiece. He died shortly before the first performance.

MAIN COMPOSITIONS opera: *The Tales of Hoffman* (1881); about 100 operettas including *Orphée aux Enfers* (1858), *La Belle Hélène* (1865), *La Vie Parisienne* (1866), *La Grande Duchesse de Gerolstein* (1867); dances; songs.

PAGANINI, NICCOLÒ (1782–1840), was an Italian violinist who did more than any other man to extend the technique of fiddle playing. His remarkable skill led credulous people to believe he was in league with the Devil, and he was enough of a showman to play up to this, emphasising his lean and faintly satanic appearance to give colour to the legends. His life was a succession of concert tours, love affairs, and gambling. Though reputed to be tight-fisted, Paganini gave generously to fellow musicians.

Paganini's compositions were designed largely to show off his own skill, and it is as virtuoso pieces rather than music that they are now remembered. But he had a gift of melody, and several composers, including JOHANNES BRAHMS and FRANZ LISZT, have used his themes for sets of variations.

MAIN COMPOSITIONS 5 violin concertos, many violin solos; chamber music including guitar quartets.

PALESTRINA, GIOVANNI PIERLUIGI DA (*c.* 1525–94), was a leading Italian composer of Church music, and took part in reforming it. In his work he stands midway between the simple choral music of earlier generations and the elaborate music of the time of J. S. BACH. He was born at Palestrina, a town near Rome from which he took his name. As a boy he became a choirboy at the church of Santa Maria Maggiore in Rome. After his voice broke he returned to Palestrina as organist and singer at the cathedral. Six years later the Bishop of Palestrina was elected Pope as Julius III, and the new Pope soon sent for Palestrina to become *maestro di cappella* of the Julian Chapel at the Vatican.

In 1576 Pope Gregory XIII commissioned Palestrina and a fellow musician, Annibale Zoilo, to produce a reformed version of the plainsong of the Mass—that is, the Church's official music, as distinct from the many other Mass settings that were written. Palestrina spent some time on this work, but then gave up the task as hopeless, and returned to the composition of new music. Palestrina's music was widely regarded in his own time as ideal for the Church that he served. For this view his skill in allowing the words their due importance, and not permitting the music to overpower them, is probably largely responsible. He maintained a careful balance between melody and harmony, and displayed a wide variety in his ways of setting the words of the Mass and the other religious texts that he used. He also wrote secular vocal works, and was one of the earliest musicians to set sonnets in madrigal form.

MAIN COMPOSITIONS 105 Masses; more than 250 motets; Magnificats; hymns; madrigals.

PARRY, SIR (CHARLES) HUBERT HASTINGS (1848–1918), was one of the dominant figures in English music in the late nineteenth century. He was the son of an English country gentleman, and began to write music at the age of eight. He took an Oxford University degree in music while still a schoolboy at Eton College, then continued his musical studies at Oxford and in Stuttgart. Parry began his career as a businessman, devoting all his spare time to music. In 1883 he joined the staff of the Royal College of Music, London, becoming director of the college eleven years later. In 1900 he added to his already considerable duties the post of professor of music at Oxford. Despite this busy round of teaching and administration he found time for composition, as well as for writing scholarly books on Bach and musical style and taking part in every possible form of athletics. His musical skill and integrity left a lasting impression on generations of English musicians.

Parry's own work combines a bluff, hearty Englishness with a strong streak of mysticism, perhaps shown most strongly in his setting of William Blake's *Jerusalem*, now firmly established as one of England's most patriotic songs. Although he wrote many instrumental pieces, it is his choral works and songs by which he is best remembered. He was made a baronet in 1903.

MAIN COMPOSITIONS oratorios: *Judith* (1888), *Job* (1892), *King Saul* (1894); orchestral: 5 symphonies, overtures, *Symphonic Variations* (1897); organ: choral preludes, choral fantasies, *Wanderer Toccata and Fugue;* choral: cantatas including *Blest Pair of Sirens* (1887), *Voces Clamantium* (1903), *The Love that Casteth out Fear* (1904), odes; chamber music; piano solos; songs. BOOKS *Johann Sebastian Bach* (1909), *Style in Musical Art* (1911).

**PERGOLESI, GIOVANNI BATTISTA** (1710–36), an Italian violinist, contrived in his very short life to write fifteen stage works and a great deal of Church music. He was a delicate child, lame in one leg. From the age of sixteen he studied at a Naples conservatory. He began composing as a boy, and while still a pupil at Naples produced oratorios and other sacred music. When he was twenty-one his first opera was performed, and until his death he produced a succession of operas and *intermezzi*—one act operettas performed between the acts of more serious works. A great many works are attributed to him that he did not in fact write.

MAIN COMPOSITIONS operas: *La Salustria* (1731), *Lo Frate 'nnamorato* (1732), *Il Prigionier Superbo* (1733), *Adriano in Siria* (1734), *L'Olimpiade* (1735), *Flaminio* (1735); intermezzi: *La Serva Padrona* (1733), *La Contadina Astuta* (1734); sacred music: oratorios, Masses, *Stabat Mater* (1736); chamber music

PISTON, WALTER HAMOR (born 1894), an American composer, began his career as an art student, and turned to music only after the end of World War I, in which he served in the US navy. Piston, of Italian descent, was born at Rockland, Maine. He started his musical studies at Harvard University in 1919, and later went to Paris, where he was the pupil of NADIA BOULANGER and PAUL DUKAS. When he returned to the United States he taught at Harvard, serving as professor of music from 1944 to 1960. He wrote textbooks on harmony, counterpoint, and orchestration.

Piston's work is distinguished by its perfect craftsmanship, coupled with an emotion that has a strong classical flavour. He wrote many orchestral works, but nothing for the voice. His compositions won him two Pulitzer prizes.

MAIN COMPOSITIONS ballet: *The Incredible Flutist* (1938); orchestral: 7 symphonies, concertos for violin, viola, flute, piano, suite *Three New England Sketches* (1959), *Lincoln Center Festival Overture* (1962); chamber music.

POULENC, FRANCIS (1899–1963), a pianist, was a member of the French group of composers known as *Les Six*, who included ARTHUR HONEGGER and DARIUS MILHAUD. Poulenc's music is at its best when it is witty and satirical; his harmonic structure tends to the traditional. He decided on a musical career while serving in the forces in World War I, and picked up most of his musical education after the war ended. An outstanding pianist, he went on a series of concert tours with the singer Pierre Bernac, and wrote a number of works for the piano. His large output ranged from opera to songs.

MAIN COMPOSITIONS operas: *Le Gendarme Incompris* (1920), *Les Mamelles de Tirésias* (1944), *Dialogues des Carmélites* (1957), *La Voix Humaine* (1958); ballet: *Les Biches* (1924); orchestral works including harpsichord and piano concertos; piano solos; song cycles; part-songs and solo songs.

PROKOFIEV, SERGEI SERGEEVICH (1891–1953), a brilliant pianist, was one of the leading Russian composers of the first half of the twentieth century. At twenty-three, while a student at the St Petersburg (now Leningrad) conservatory, he won a major prize for his first piano concerto. After the Russian Revolution he lived abroad for fourteen years, spending part of the time with Sergei Diaghilev's Russian ballet, for which he wrote three works. Probably his best known piece is the children's fairy tale *Peter and the Wolf*— for narrator and orchestra.

Unable to settle outside Russia, Prokofiev returned home, and for a time was regarded with favour by the Soviet authorities. But towards the end of his life he was officially censured for the 'anti-democratic tendencies' of his music, and had to promise reforms. In his early days Prokofiev was unjustly described as an *enfant terrible*, and he never really lived this reputation down. His work is largely clean-cut, lyrical, and easy to appreciate.

MAIN COMPOSITIONS operas: *The Gambler* (1929), *The Love of Three Oranges* (1921), *The Fiery Angel* (1955), *Semyon Kotko* (1940), *The Duenna* (1946), *War and Peace* (1946), *The Story of a Real Man* (1948); ballets: *The Buffoon* (1921), *Le Pas d'acier* (1927), *L'Enfant prodigue* (1929), *Sur le Borysthène* (1932), *Romeo and Juliet* (1938), *Tale of the Stone Flower* (1954); orchestral: 7 symphonies, 5 piano concertos, 2 violin concertos, cello concerto, suites *Lieutenant Kizhe* (1934), *Peter and the Wolf* (1936); piano sonatas; chamber music; film music.

# PUCCINI, GIACOMO ANTONIO DOMENICO MICH-
ELE SECONDO MARIA (1858–1924), was a great Italian
opera composer. His four immediate Puccini ancestors were
*maestri di cappella* at Lucca Cathedral, and it was intended
that Giacomo should follow his father in that post. But having
seen GIUSEPPE VERDI's *Aida* Puccini decided that his career
lay in opera. He won a subsidised place at the Milan conservatory, and while there composed a one-act opera, *Le Villi.*
He entered it for a competition unsuccessfully, but attracted
the attention of a publisher, Giulio Ricordi, who became a
lifelong friend. From then on Puccini produced a succession
of operas, nearly all of them successes.

MAIN COMPOSITIONS operas: *Le Villi* (1884), *Edgar* (1889),
*Manon Lescaut* (1893), *La Bohème* (1896), *Tosca* (1900),
*Madama Butterfly* (1904), *La Fanciulla del West* (*The Girl
of the Golden West*, 1910), *La Rondine* (1917), *Il Trittico*
(trilogy of one-act operas, 1918), *Turandot* (completed by
Franco Alfano, 1926).

# PURCELL, HENRY (1659–95), a singer and organist, was
one of England's greatest composers, and also one of the leading composers of his time. He was born just before the Res-
toration of the English monarchy after the austerities of the
Cromwellian era, and grew to manhood in the shadow of the
cultured, pleasure-loving court of Charles II. His father,
Thomas Purcell, was a court musician, a Gentleman of the
Chapel Royal and an official composer. From him Purcell
received his musical education, and through his influence
became a boy chorister in the Chapel Royal. At eighteen his
outstanding talents brought him a coveted post: Composer
in Ordinary for the king's string orchestra. Two years later
he was made organist of Westminster Abbey.

In his early years he wrote a series of fantasias for strings
and also some sets of sonatas for two violins which are among
the finest of their kind. As court composer he was kept busy
writing music for special occasions—birthday odes, coronation anthems, and *Te Deums*. But undoubtedly much of his

finest music was written for the stage. He suffered from the fact that there was no established opera house in London in his day; as a result much of his work in this field was incidental music for spoken drama. He produced only one true opera, *Dido and Aeneas*, which is a masterpiece. It was written for a girls' school at Chelsea. But several of his other stage works, such as *The Fairy Queen*, may be counted as operas too in spite of the great amount of dialogue they contain.

MAIN COMPOSITIONS operas and stage works: *Dido and Aeneas* (1689), *Dioclesian* (1690), *King Arthur* (1691), *The Fairy Queen* (1692); sacred music: Church services, anthems, hymns, psalms, *Te Deums*; secular choral works: cantatas, odes; instrumental: fantasias, 22 sonatas for two violins and continuo, harpsichord solos; songs.

QUANTZ, JOHANN JOACHIM (1697–1773), was a German flute virtuoso, and one of the finest writers for the instrument. He was the son of a blacksmith, who wanted him to follow his own trade. But from the age of eight Quantz showed strong musical talent, and he was able to study music as an apprentice to the musical director of Merseburg. He learned several instruments, and became an oboe player at the court of the king of Poland in 1718. Seeing no future as an oboist he took up the flute. From 1724 to 1727 he was able to visit Italy, France, and England, where he broadened his musical knowledge and met many of the leading composers of the day, including DOMENICO SCARLATTI and GEORGE FRIDERIC HANDEL.

Quantz returned to his duties in Poland in 1727. During a visit to Berlin the following year he attracted the attention of the crown prince, Frederick, who took flute lessons from him twice a year for the next thirteen years. When Frederick became king of Prussia in 1741 he persuaded Quantz to settle in Berlin as court composer on generous financial terms. For the rest of his life Quantz remained in the service of the king —better known to history as Frederick the Great.

Quantz's main duties were to conduct court concerts, and

to write flute music for the king to play. He wrote more than 300 concertos for one and two flutes, few of which have ever been published, though the manuscripts remain. Most of his other work consists of chamber music, of which he wrote a considerable amount. Quantz made several mechanical improvements to the crude flutes of his day. He also wrote a textbook on flute-playing, which was first published in 1752 and has been reprinted many times since. It is a valuable work for the light it throws on the music of the time.

MAIN COMPOSITIONS 300 flute concertos; chamber music including flute solos, trios, and quartets; songs.

RACHMANINOV, SERGEI VASILIEVICH (1873–1943), a Russian pianist, won world-wide acclaim for his virtuoso performances, and for his many piano compositions, his second piano concerto being one of the most popular ever written. The son of an army officer, Rachmaninov began his musical career early, scoring an international success at the age of twenty with his Prelude in C♯ minor. After the Russian Revolution of 1917 he emigrated, and settled in the United States, spending most of his time as a pianist.

Rachmaninov's music is strongly romantic in character, tinged always with a characteristic Russian melancholy. For a time it was banned by the Communist rulers of Russia as representing the 'decadence of the lower middle classes'.

MAIN COMPOSITIONS operas: *Aleko* (1893), *The Miserly Knight* (1906), *Francesco da Rimini* (1906); orchestral: 3 symphonies, choral symphony *The Bells* (1913), 3 symphonic dances, 4 piano concertos, *Rhapsody on a Theme by Paganini* for piano and orchestra; chamber music; piano solos; songs.

RAMEAU, JEAN PHILIPPE (1683–1764), an organist and harpsichord player, was the principal French composer of his day. His father, an organist, intended him to be a lawyer, but Rameau would not learn anything except music. As a youth he travelled in Italy, returning to France with a troupe of actors. He then took a series of appointments as a cathedral organist, spending much of his spare time writing two important books on harmony and musical theory. These books served as the foundations of modern musical theory.

About the time his harmony book was published, Rameau settled in Paris, where he spent the rest of his life. His theoretical works established him as a teacher, and for a while he gave up his career as an organist. About this time, too, he married a singer some twenty-five years his junior. His great ambition was to write operas, but he had no success in this field until he met a wealthy patron of the arts, La Riche de la Pouplinière. La Pouplinière at once realised Rameau's gifts and appointed him music master and conductor of his private orchestra. This gave Rameau time and facilities for composition.

Rameau produced his first important opera, *Hippolyte et Aricie*, in 1733, when he was fifty years old, at a period when the average expectation of life was only forty years. He continued writing and producing operas for the rest of his days. In between he wrote pamphlets in defence of his musical ideas, which were bitterly attacked by his many enemies, among them Jean-Jacques Rousseau, the philosopher, who was also a musician. Ironically, Rameau, who was accused in his earlier days of being too Italian in his work, became the chief defender of French music against the new Italian works favoured by Rousseau and others.

MAIN COMPOSITIONS operas: *Hippolyte et Aricie* (1733), *Les Indes Galantes* (1735), *Castor et Pollux* (1737), *Festes d'Hébé* (1739), *Dardanus* (1739), *La Princesse de Navarre* (1745), *Zoroastre* (1749); harpsichord solos (3 books); chamber music; motets; cantatas. MAIN BOOKS *Traité de l'harmonie reduite à ses principes naturels* (1722), *Nouveau système de musique théorique* (1726).

RAVEL, MAURICE JOSEPH (1875–1937), brought to French music an originality of thought that may have been due in part to his ancestry—a mixture of Swiss and Basque. Ravel made his reputation at the age of twenty-four with his piano solo *Pavane pour une infante défunte*. He produced a stream of compositions, all characterised by a precise attention to detail and to form and craftsmanship.

His music marks a reaction from the heavy, rich textures of RICHARD WAGNER and his followers. It includes some fine chamber music, the ballet *Daphnis et Chloé*, written for the ballet master Serge Diaghilev, and two operas. Ravel's orchestral music, however, which included such masterpieces as *Boléro* and *Rapsodie espagnole* (both showing the influences of his Spanish connections), must be ranked among his greatest. During World War I he served as an air force ambulance driver, but was wounded and invalided out with a nervous disorder which never left him. He found some comfort in the hobby of collecting mechanical toys.

MAIN COMPOSITIONS operas: *L'Heure espagnole* (1907), *L'Enfant et les sortilèges* (1925); ballets: *Daphnis et Chloé* (1912), *La Valse* (1920); orchestral: *Rapsodie espagnole* (1907), *Boléro* (1927), 2 piano concertos (one for left hand); chamber music; piano works: *Pavane pour une infante défunte* (1899), *Jeux d'eau* (1901), *Gaspard de la nuit* (1908), *Valses nobles et sentimentales* (1911), suite, *Ma Mère l'Oye* (1911, as a ballet 1915), *Le Tombeau de Couperin* (1917); songs and song cycles.

RESPIGHI, OTTORINO (1879–1936), an Italian violinist, violist and teacher, is remembered in his own country for his operas, and outside it for his descriptive orchestral works, such as the suites *Fontane di Roma* and *Pini di Roma*. As a young man he went to St Petersburg (now Leningrad); there he studied with NIKOLAI RIMSKY-KORSAKOV while earning his living as a violist in the opera orchestra. Later he studied in Berlin with MAX BRUCH. At the age of thirty-four he was appointed professor of composition at the Rome conservatory. Respighi made a number of arrangements of other music, the most successful being the ballet *La Boutique Fantasque*, from pieces by GIOACCHINO ROSSINI.

MAIN COMPOSITIONS operas: *Re Enzo* (1905), *Semiråma*

(1910), *Belfagor* (1923), *Maria Egiziaca* (1932), *La Fiamma* (1934), *Lucrezia* (1937); ballets; orchestral: *Fontane di Roma, Pini di Roma, Vetrate di chiesa*, concertos; chamber music; songs.

RIMSKY-KORSAKOV, NIKOLAI ANDREEVICH (1844–1908), a Russian naval officer, became one of his country's most important nationalist composers, and a master of orchestration. While still at naval college he met MILI BALAKIREV and under his influence began to study music. He became a leading member of the group of composers known as 'The Five', all of whom were at first amateur musicians while following other careers.

During a three-year naval cruise Rimsky-Korsakov wrote his first symphony, which was also the first by a Russian composer. As a result of his work he was offered the post of professor of composition at the St Petersburg (now Leningrad) conservatory, which he took. Two years later he left the navy after seventeen years' service—most of it a mere sinecure— to devote his full time to his new post. In the next few years he held a number of official positions, while composing a great deal of fine music. His many pupils included ALEKSANDR GLAZUNOV, IGOR STRAVINSKY and OTTORINO RESPIGHI.

In his late forties Rimsky-Korsakov had a spell during which music became distasteful to him, but it lasted only a couple of years. During the revolution of 1905 he fell foul of the authorities, and was dismissed from the conservatory with a ban on his music. But he was soon reinstated and became more popular than ever. He helped to finish and revise works by his friends, ALEKSANDR BORODIN and MODESTE MUSSORGSKY, and though he has been criticised for the changes he made he kept the works from oblivion.

Rimsky-Korsakov was strongly influenced by RICHARD WAGNER and by Russian folk music. Much of his finest and most popular music is in his operas, including the perennial favourite 'The Flight of the Bumble Bee' from *The Tale of Tsar Saltan*. He wrote an important treatise on orchestration.

MAIN COMPOSITIONS operas: *The Maid of Pskov (Ivan the Terrible*, 1873), *A Night in May* (1880), *The Snow Maiden* (1882), *Christmas Eve* (1895), *Mlada* (1892), *Sadko* (1898), *Mozart and Salieri* (1898), *The Tsar's Bride* (1899), *The Tale of Tsar Saltan* (1900), *Kashchei the Immortal* (1902), *Pan Voyevoda* (1904), *The Invisible City of Kitezh* (1907), *The Golden Cockerel* (1909); orchestral: 3 symphonies; piano concerto, *Capriccio Espagnol, Scheherazade, Russian Easter Overture*; chamber music; piano works; songs.

ROSSINI, GIOACCHINO ANTONIO (1792–1868), one of the greatest Italian opera composers, was the son of an opera singer and the town trumpeter of Pesaro, who combined this post with that of inspector of slaughterhouses. In 1810 his first opera, *La Cambiale di Matrimonio*, was produced in Venice. Three years later the warm and expressive melodies of *Tancredi* won him fame not just in Italy but in all Europe. From then on his success was assured, despite occasional individual failures. His masterpiece, *Il Barbiere di Seviglia*, was hissed on its first night in 1816, but was soon drawing packed houses. He composed it in just two weeks.

By the time he was thirty-one Rossini had written more than thirty operas. He began to travel, and after meeting LUDWIG VAN BEETHOVEN in Vienna and visiting London, he moved to Paris as director of the Théâtre Italien and court composer to the French king. In 1829 he produced there his most famous opera, *Guillaume Tell*. At that moment, when he was thirty-seven, wealthy, with the world at his feet, he stopped composing. For the remainder of his life he lived quietly, teaching, and writing only two major works, a *Stabat Mater* and a Mass. His health was poor, and it is probable that composing had lost its interest for him. His famous remark 'Give me a laundry list and I'll set it to music' suggests it was too easy to be fun any more. In his later years he wrote a series of occasional pieces which he called 'The sins of old age', and from which OTTORINO RESPIGHI later made the ballet *La Boutique Fantasque*.

MAIN COMPOSITIONS more than 40 operas, including *La Cambiale di Matrimonio* (1810), *Tancredi* (1813), *L'Italiana in Algeri* (1813), *Il Barbiere di Seviglia* (1816), *Otello* (1816), *La Gazza Ladra* (*The Thieving Magpie*, 1817), *Semiramide* (1823), *Le Comte Ory* (1828), *Guillaume Tell* (1829); religious works: *Stabat Mater* (1839), *Petite Messe solennelle* (1864); chamber music; songs.

SAINT-SAËNS, (CHARLES) CAMILLE (1835–1921), a French virtuoso organist and pianist, was a prolific composer who is remembered chiefly for his *Carnaval des animaux* for two pianos and orchestra, and for his symphonic poems. A child prodigy (he was playing the piano at two), he went to the Paris conservatory at fourteen, and produced his first symphony at eighteen. FRANZ LISZT, from whom he adopted the symphonic poem, heard him play at the age of twenty-two and called him the world's finest organist. He aspired to write operas, but of the dozen he wrote only one, *Samson et Dalila*, is still performed. Saint-Saëns loved foreign travel, and was an urbane and witty person who enjoyed both his work and his leisure.

MAIN COMPOSITIONS operas: *Samson et Dalila* (1877); orchestral: 3 symphonies, symphonic poems *Le Rouet d'Omphale*, *Phaëton*, *Danse Macabre*, *La Jeunesse d'Hercule*, concertos for piano, cello, and violin, *Carnaval des animaux* (1886); chamber music; choral music.

SATIE, ERIC ALFRED LESLIE (1866–1925), known as *Erik Satie*, was one of the most original and eccentric of French composers. His mother was Scottish, and both his parents were musicians. He began his musical career with a year's conventional study at the Paris conservatory, then became a pianist in a café. At this time the heavy influence of Wagner was strong in French music. Satie took a perverse delight in doing things differently, and the whimsical side of his nature obscured his very real interest in original thought and development.

Satie's scores—written without bar lines in red ink—abound with odd titles such as *Limp Preludes for a Dog, Things Seen to Right and Left (Without Spectacles)*, and *Pearshaped Pieces*. The more conservative of his contemporaries were baffled by these eccentricities, as they were by his, to their ears, strange harmonies. But he had considerable influence on many others, notably MAURICE RAVEL and the group of composers known as *Les Six*—who included ARTHUR HONNEGER, DARIUS MILHAUD, and FRANCIS POULENC. He was a close friend of CLAUDE DEBUSSY, who, though not influenced by him, encouraged him in his experiments. At the age of thirty-nine Satie decided to extend his formal knowledge of music, and spent three years in the Schola Cantorum in Paris under the guidance of VINCENT D'INDY.

MAIN COMPOSITIONS ballets: *Parade* (1916), *Mercure* (1924), *Relâche* (1924); vocal: *Messe des pauvres* (1895), *Socrate* (1918); orchestral works; piano pieces.

SCARLATTI, (PIETRO) ALESSANDRO GASPARE (1660–1725), was in his time one of the most prolific composers of operas, of which he wrote 115 (seventy still survive). His importance now is largely as one of the developers of classical harmony. At the age of nineteen he won the patronage of the former Queen Christina of Sweden, then living in Rome, and from then on never lacked for wealthy patrons and lucrative posts. In his operas he developed the *da capo* aria and also widened the scope and use of the orchestra, using wind instruments for special effects. One of his pupils was his son, DOMENICO SCARLATTI.

MAIN COMPOSITIONS 115 operas, including *Mitradate Eupatore* (1707), *Il trionfo del' onore* (1718); 10 masses; chamber music; serenades; 692 chamber cantatas; madrigals.

SCARLATTI, (GIUSEPPE) DOMENICO (1685–1757), son and pupil of ALESSANDRO SCARLATTI, was one of the greatest harpsichord players of his day. At the age of twenty, with at least one opera already to his credit, he went to Venice to

97

continue his studies. Later in Rome he met GEORGE FRIDERIC HANDEL, who was his own age, and the two young men became fast friends. Scarlatti, an easy-going and modest man, always spoke reverently of Handel's playing if anyone praised his own. Scarlatti held a number of posts, one of these being at Lisbon where the Princess Maria Barbara was his pupil. When Maria Barbara married the heir to the Spanish throne, Scarlatti went to Spain in her service and remained there for the rest of his life, apart from visits to England and Ireland. An inveterate gambler, he was often hard up in his later years.

Musically, Scarlatti is important for his brilliant harpsichord works, which laid the foundations of modern keyboard technique. He wrote well over 550 of these pieces, which are generally called sonatas, though most of them are comparatively short pieces and not true sonatas. Some idea of their technical demands can be gained from his remark that since he had ten fingers and the instrument could employ them all, he saw no reason why he should not use them.

MAIN COMPOSITIONS 13 operas; oratorios and cantatas; 550 harpsichord sonatas.

SCHÖNBERG, ARNOLD (1874–1951), an Austrian-born teacher, was probably the most influential composer of the twentieth century. He learned the violin and cello as a boy, but did not adopt music as a career until he was twenty-one, working at first as a bank clerk. As a composer he was largely self taught. At first he was influenced by the music of JOHANNES BRAHMS and RICHARD WAGNER, though even in his earliest works he was experimenting with problems of tonality—the relationship of a piece of music to a definite key note. He married at the age of twenty-seven, and for many years his musical career was largely a struggle to make a living, conducting in cabarets and orchestrating other people's music. Then he secured a post in a Berlin conservatory as a teacher.

When he was thirty-four Schönberg began writing completely atonal music, that is, music with no key note. His atonal period lasted for about fifteen years. At this time he was associated with a group of Munich artists who called themselves 'Der Blaue Reiter' (the Blue Rider), and himself painted some pictures. Schönberg's new-style music aroused great hostility: the first performance of his *Pierrot Lunaire* for voice and instruments at Berlin in 1912 led to catcalls and fighting in the audience, and there were similar scenes when his *Five Pieces for Orchestra* were performed in London the same year. Altogether, the music of Schönberg and his two principal pupils, ANTON WEBERN and ALBAN BERG, aroused great interest and criticism.

In 1920 Schönberg began experimenting with a new system of composition, variously known as the twelve-tone, note-row, or serial method. In this, a composition could be built up from an arrangement or note row, generally the twelve semitones of the chromatic scale arranged in a pre-determined order. He used this method of composition for the next few years, though later he also wrote a number of works employing definite keys.

At the age of fifty-two he was appointed to a senior teaching post at the Prussian Academy of Arts in Berlin, but was dismissed after seven years by the new Nazi rulers of Germany because he was Jewish. Schönberg had become a Christian some years earlier, but when he was dismissed he returned to the Jewish faith. He left Germany and settled in the United States, in due course becoming an American citizen and adopting the spelling Schoenberg for his name.

Schönberg's influence on many later composers has proved to be of greater importance than his own music, valuable though that is. Among his many critics was JEAN SIBELIUS, who once said: 'There are not twenty musicians in the world who could follow the structure and inner logic of any recent Schönberg work... I have to study the score closely to see what he is driving at.'

MAIN COMPOSITIONS operas: *Erwartung* (1924), *Von Heute auf Morgen* (1930), *Moses und Aron* (1957), *Die glückliche Hand* (1924); orchestral and vocal: *Pierrot Lunaire* (1912), *Five Pieces for Orchestra* (1912), *Kammersymphonie* (1913), concertos for piano and violin; chamber music; piano solos; songs.

SCHUBERT, FRANZ PETER (1797–1828), one of the many composers who lived in Vienna, was one of the few to be born there. He was already composing at a considerable rate when he became a schoolmaster at the age of seventeen. The next year of Schubert's life was one of the most remarkable. While working as a teacher he produced two symphonies, six operas, two Masses, three sonatas, and almost 150 songs to poems by the German writer Johann von Goethe. His ability to put notes on paper was remarkable, and it is said that he sometimes failed to recognise his own work when it was shown to him at a later date.

Schubert spent almost four years as a schoolmaster, loathing the drudgery of it. At last he broke free, and after a summer spent as music tutor to the children of Count Esterházy settled down in Vienna among a circle of congenial friends. With their aid he supported himself as best he could, occasionally selling some of his prodigious output of music to publishers, or teaching. He spent much time with his friends, drinking wine in taverns or, more often, sitting over a cup of coffee in Bogner's Coffee House, where he would gaze admiringly at Vienna's greatest musician, BEETHOVEN.

At the age of twenty-five he contracted a serious illness which lingered for about a year, leaving him weakened and unhappy. He recovered, though not completely, and the flow of compositions continued almost unabated. He made several attempts to break into the world of opera, but without success. Meanwhile his reputation was growing steadily. In 1827 Schubert carried a torch at Beethoven's funeral, and then in company with some friends drank a toast to the one who should most quickly follow Beethoven to the grave. A year later to the day he gave his first public concert, and from it made enough money to buy a piano. But his health was no better, and a few months later he contracted typhoid fever from drinking polluted water, and died.

Schubert's music is uneven. He wrote at such a rate that some of his output is humdrum, and the movements of some of his works are too long to be enjoyable. But he was a master of melody, and one of the greatest writers of songs the world has yet seen. In his symphonies and his chamber music he developed gradually a depth of feeling that showed a growing maturity, and he died before his powers had reached their full height.

MAIN COMPOSITIONS 4 operas, and 5 operettas; orchestral: 9 symphonies (2 incomplete), overtures; Church music: Masses, *Magnificats*, *Kyries*; other choral works: cantatas, part songs; chamber music; piano solos and duets; 600 songs; song cycles.

SCHUMANN, ROBERT ALEXANDER (1810–56), was one of the most literary of musicians. By his writings he did much to help the Romantic movement in music, and in his own compositions he was among the most Romantic of them all. As a person he was shy and inarticulate, but he 'spoke' freely with his pen. He went to Leipzig University to study law, but spent more time on music. He had piano lessons from an outstanding teacher, Friedrich Wieck, and hoped to become a concert pianist. After transferring for a time to Heidelberg University Schumann settled down to work at the piano, and devised a machine to strengthen a weak finger. Misuse of the machine resulted in permanent damage, and he found that he could no longer hope to be a pianist. He was determined not to be a lawyer, and decided to devote his time to composition and journalism.

With some friends Schumann founded *Die neue Zeitschrift für Musik* (*The New Music Magazine*), which he edited for ten years. For it he created a largely imaginary group of musicians which he called *Die Davidsbündler* (David's Band). Two of the characters in it, Florestan and Eusebius, represented two aspects of Schumann's own character. In the magazine Schumann did a great deal to encourage new and original music, and to attack what he regarded as the 'philistines' who opposed all things new. At the same time Schumann himself was producing a quantity of music, much of it for piano.

Meanwhile he had fallen in love with Wieck's daughter Clara, nine years his junior. Wieck refused his consent to their marriage on the grounds that Schumann was a heavy drinker. But he relented after the couple sought the aid of the courts. With Clara's encouragement Schumann widened the field of his compositions, writing songs, orchestral works, chamber music, and even oratorio.

At the age of forty Schumann obtained a post as conductor at Düsseldorf. He held it for three years, during which he wrote a great deal of music. But his shortcomings as a conductor led to friction, and he was asked to give up conducting anything except his own works. At this time the Schumanns had a visit from a young musician, JOHANNES BRAHMS, in whom Schumann's keen critical faculties at once discerned a future greatness. But Schumann's mind was now seriously affected; at his own request he was placed in an asylum for the insane, having tried to commit suicide.

MAIN COMPOSITIONS opera: *Genoveva* (1850); oratorio: *Paradise and the Peri* (1843); orchestral: 4 symphonies, overtures, concertos for piano, cello; choral works; chamber music; piano solos; songs.

SCHÜTZ, HEINRICH (1585–1672), Germany's leading composer of the seventeenth century, began his career as a lawyer but soon turned to music, and studied with GIOVANNI GABRIELI in Venice. He spent most of his life as *Kapellmeister* to the Elector of Saxony at Dresden, though with visits to Italy. On one of these it is thought he may have studied with CLAUDIO MONTEVERDI.

Schütz wrote some Italian madrigals and the first ever German opera, *Daphne* (now lost). All the rest of his known works are vocal compositions for the Church, in which the influence of Monteverdi shows. Schütz was able to combine the richness of the Italian style with the more austere traditions of Germany's Lutheran Church. He developed the oratorio, and wrote three *Passions* that foreshadow those of Bach.

MAIN COMPOSITIONS opera: *Daphne* (1627); oratorios; *Cantiones Sacrae*; *Symphoniae Sacrae* (1629, 1647, 1650); 3 *Passions*; madrigals.

SCRIABIN, ALEKSANDR NIKOLAEVICH (1872–1915), a Russian piano virtuoso, began his career—like several other Russian musicians—as an army cadet. He studied music at the same time, and music won as a career. After several years touring Europe he married a fellow pianist and settled down as a professor at the Moscow conservatory. When he was thirty-two he moved for a time to Switzerland, where he gave all his time to mysticism, theosophy, and composition.

Scriabin's ideas have been described as embodying 'a sort of philosophical programme music'. They included many harmonic innovations, and in the orchestral work *Prometheus* he added a part for a colour organ to throw coloured lights on to a screen during the performance. Scriabin planned a major work in which music, light, perfume, and dancing were to be combined in a sort of religious ecstasy, but he died before he could complete it.

MAIN COMPOSITIONS orchestral: three symphonies, *Poem of ecstasy* (1908), *Prometheus* (1911), piano concerto; piano solos.

SESSIONS, ROGER HUNTINGTON (born 1896), an American teacher, co-operated with AARON COPLAND in actively encouraging the development of American music. He was born in Brooklyn, and after studying at Harvard University and the Yale School of Music spent eight years in further study in Europe, interspersed with visits to his homeland. Between 1928 and 1931 he and Copland organised a festival series, the Copland–Sessions concerts, to bring modern music to the notice of the American public. His teaching appointments were with Princeton University and the University of California, and at the Juilliard School of Music in New York City.

103

Sessions' musical output is relatively small, probably because of his commitment to teaching. A serious-minded composer, many of his works are on a grand scale, such as the Second Symphony, dedicated on its first performance in 1946 to the memory of President Franklin D. Roosevelt who died the year before. The symphony also marks the transition of Sessions' music to the twelve-tone style of ARNOLD SCHÖNBERG, his earlier works having been tonal.

MAIN COMPOSITIONS operas: *The Trial of Lucullus* (1947), *Montezuma* (1964); orchestral: 5 symphonies, suites; chamber music; piano solos.

SHOSTAKOVICH, DIMITRI DIMITRIEVICH (born 1906), became the leading and 'approved' composer of the Communist era in the Soviet Union. He wrote his first symphony while still a student, and because of its international success he decided to make composition his career (he had earlier planned to be a solo pianist). His gift for parody and comedy was not appreciated by the Soviet authorities, who denounced his second opera, *A Lady Macbeth of Mtsensk*, as 'muddle, not music'— although he had written it in accordance with Joseph Stalin's ruling that music should express 'The ideas and passions motivating Soviet heroes'.

After a spell out of favour Shostakovich won renewed support with his fifth symphony, and remained in high regard until 1948, when he was publicly rebuked for 'anti-popular tendencies'. Equally publicly he repented and promised to conform. Eight years later he was back in favour. His music, which owes something to that of PETR TCHAIKOVSKY and NIKOLAI RIMSKY-KORSAKOV, shows the difficulties of reconciling his natural pungent wit with the more solid and stolid requirements of Soviet musical ideology. In spite of this he won the Stalin prize five times, and the Lenin prize once, and was awarded the Order of Lenin.

MAIN COMPOSITIONS operas: *The Nose* (1930), *A Lady Macbeth of Mtsensk* (1934), *Moscow, Cheremushki* (1959); ballets: *The Golden Age* (1930), *Bolt* (1931), *Bright Rivulet*

(1935); orchestral: symphonies, suites, symphonic poems, concertos for piano, violin, and cello; choral works; chamber music; piano solos; song cycles; film scores.

SIBELIUS, JEAN (1865–1957), Finland's greatest musician, was also one of the outstanding composers of the twentieth century. He was the son of an army doctor, and was given the names *Johan Julius Christian*; but he later adopted the French form of his first name, Jean, and used it thenceforward. At first Sibelius studied law, but soon abandoned it in favour of music. When he was twenty-four he went to Berlin to study, and from there moved to Vienna. He returned to Finland when he was twenty-seven, and soon afterwards the performances of his first major works, the choral symphony *Kullervo* and the tone-poem *En Saga,* made his reputation. When he was thirty-two the Finnish government gave him a small life pension so that he could devote his time to composition. Two years later he produced possibly his most famous tone poem, the patriotic *Finlandia.*

Sibelius made some foreign tours as a conductor; then for five years he was dogged by ear trouble. In 1904 he moved from Finland's capital, Helsinki, to the village of Järvenpää, some 56km (35 miles) away on the shores of Lake Tuusula. There, in his home, 'Ainola', he spent the next twenty-five years composing, producing a succession of superb works, culminating in his fifth, sixth, and seventh symphonies and the tone poem *Tapiola.* Tapio is the god of the forests in Finnish mythology, and this work, like many others written by Sibelius, evokes the atmosphere and spirit of Finland, with its thousands of forests and lakes.

MAIN COMPOSITIONS orchestral: 7 symphonies, tone poems *En Saga* (1892), *The Swan of Tuonela* (1893), *Finlandia* (1899), *Night-Ride and Sunrise* (1909), *Tapiola* (1926), overtures, suite *Karelia* (1893), marches; concerto and other works for violin; chamber music; organ solos; piano solos; incidental music; choral music: *Kullervo* (1892), cantatas, part songs; songs.

SMETANA, BEDŘICH (1824–84), a pianist, conductor, and teacher, was one of the first great Czech composers. Outside his own country he is known chiefly for his opera *The Bartered Bride*. The son of a brewer, he resisted attempts to make him follow his father's occupation, and devoted all his efforts to music. At the age of nineteen he went to Prague, and was lucky enough to be appointed music teacher to a wealthy household, a post he held for about five years. Then, with help from FRANZ LISZT, he set up a music school and married a fellow musician. Eight years later he went to Göteborg, Sweden, as conductor of the philharmonic society there. During his five years in Sweden he lost his first wife, but soon married again.

At the age of thirty-seven he became the first conductor and principal composer of a new opera house in Prague, and produced a series of operas that brought him fame and a comfortable position. But when he was fifty he became totally deaf, and had to resign all his appointments. For several years he was able to carry on composing, but gradually his mind too became affected.

MAIN COMPOSITIONS operas: *The Brandenburgers in Bohemia* (1866), *The Bartered Bride* (1866), *Dalibor* (1868), *Libuše* (1881), *The Two Widows* (1874), *The Kiss* (1876), *The Secret* (1878); orchestral: symphonic poems *Má vlast* (*My Country*); chamber music; piano solos.

SOUSA, JOHN PHILIP (1854–1932), an American bandmaster, was an outstanding composer of military marches. He is often known as 'the March King'. Sousa was born in Washington, DC, the son of a Portuguese immigrant who had married a German. His father was a trombone player, and Sousa Junior studied that instrument as well as the violin, playing both instruments in orchestras as a young man. In 1880 he was appointed conductor of the United States Marine Band, and in the twelve years in which he led it he raised it to a high degree of performance. He left the Marines to form his own band, which he took on tour all over the world.

In addition to his many military marches, Sousa wrote operettas, textbooks on the trumpet and violin, and novels. His anthology *National, Patriotic and Typical Airs of all Countries,* published in 1890, was compiled for the US Navy.

MAIN COMPOSITIONS 13 operettas: *El Capitán* (1896); 140 military marches, including *Hail to the Spirit of Liberty, King Cotton, The Liberty Bell, Semper Fidelis, The Stars and Stripes Forever, The Thunderer, The Washington Post.*

SPOHR, LOUIS (1784–1859), a German violin virtuoso and opera conductor, was regarded by some of his contemporaries as a greater composer than LUDWIG VAN BEETHOVEN. He is today remembered chiefly for one of his violin concertos, and for some chamber music. A child genius, he received a thorough training on the violin, though he seems to have picked up most of his knowledge of composition from studying the works of MOZART. His musical education was paid for by the Duke of Brunswick, who appointed him to his court band. In 1804 he set out on a visit to Paris, during which he lost his precious Guarnerius del Gesù violin. It was stolen from his carriage, and has never been seen since.

The following year Spohr became leader of the band to the Duke of Gotha, and married Dorette Scheidler, a young harpist. They appeared at concerts together for many years. In 1812 Spohr moved to Vienna as director of the Theater an der Wien. During the next few years he made many concert tours as a violinist and conductor, eventually settling for the rest of his life at the court of Kassel, where he was appointed conductor. He was able to make further tours during his annual vacations.

Spohr's reputation as a violinist was closely rivalled by his fame as a composer, especially of operas. He was one of the earliest of the German Romantic composers, but his talents were strictly limited. Though he was always ready to experiment with new combinations of instruments and the writing

107

of programme music, his style and ideas remained always the same. This mannerism has contributed to his present neglect.

Spohr's own judgment of other music was often faulty. He could not understand the works of WEBER or the later symphonies of Beethoven. He once asked a pupil who had just played one of Beethoven's piano sonatas: 'Have you composed much more in that style?' But he was one of the early champions of RICHARD WAGNER, and conducted performances of two of his operas. He wrote an important treatise on violin playing.

MAIN COMPOSITIONS 10 operas including *Faust* (1816), *Zemire und Azor* (1819), *Jessonda* (1823), *Die Kreuzfahrer* (1845); orchestral: 9 symphonies, overtures, concertos for violin, harp, clarinet; choral: 4 oratorios, a Mass, cantatas; chamber music; songs and part-songs.

STOCKHAUSEN, KARLHEINZ (born 1928), a German theoretician and teacher, became one of the principal exponents of electronic music, written under the influence of the twelve-note system of ARNOLD SCHÖNBERG. After studying with OLIVIER MESSIAEN and DARIUS MILHAUD, Stockhausen became interested in *musique concrète,* in which sounds naturally produced are processed by means of tape recorders to produce new and often strangely beautiful effects. From this he progressed to a study of music composed on a basis of sounds generated electronically, and founded a studio in Cologne to produce such music. He studied the scientific aspects of musical sound in an endeavour to relate his works to their origins. Influenced possibly by such free composers as JOHN CAGE, his later works give a high degree of freedom to the performer.

Stockhausen's influence on later composers has been very great, and his work has served to open up a whole new range of tonal and dynamic possibilities. With all his innovations, he has used the classical device of counterpoint to superimpose strands of sound one upon the other, sometimes to a predetermined plan, sometimes largely at random. He has also blended western, oriental, and African musical themes in his work to produce a new truly international style.

MAIN COMPOSITIONS instrumental and orchestral: *Kontrapunkte* (1952), *Zeitmasse* (1956), *Gruppen* (1959); choral: *Carré* (1960), *Momente* (1958); electronic: *Elektronische Studien* (1953), *Kontakte* (1960), *Teletape* (1966), *Mikrophonie II* (1969); piano solos *Klavierstücke I-XI*.

STRAUSS, JOHANN (1825–99), known as Johann Strauss the Younger to distinguish him from his father, became known as 'The Waltz King' because of the many delightful waltzes (more than 150) that he wrote. Johann the Elder (1804–1849), born in Vienna, became a conductor and a prolific composer of waltzes, polkas, and other dances. He formed his own orchestra, and toured Europe with it. He put his eldest son, Johann II, into a bank, but Johann II quietly formed his own orchestra and was soon rivalling his father. On the older man's death Johann combined their orchestras, which he conducted for some years. Eventually he handed over the orchestra to his younger brothers Josef and Eduard to allow himself more time for composition.

When he was in his forties Johann II took to composing operettas, of which *Die Fledermaus* and *Die Zigeunerbaron* remain perenially popular. His most famous composition is the waltz *The Blue Danube* (1867), which to many people sums up the spirit of nineteenth-century Vienna.

MAIN COMPOSITIONS operas: *Die Karneval in Rom* (1873), *Die Fledermaus* (1874), *Eine Nacht in Venedig* (1883), *Die Ziegeunerbaron* (*The Gipsy Baron*, 1885); waltzes, polkas, and other dances.

STRAUSS, RICHARD GEORG (1864–1949), a German conductor, was one of the last of the Romantic composers, and remained so until the end of his life, despite the change that was going on all around him. He held a number of conducting posts, and at the age of forty-five he settled at

Garmisch-Partenkirchen, in Bavaria, where he was able to devote his time to writing music, interspersed with foreign tours. For a while he was director of the Vienna opera. In the 1930s he ran foul of the Nazis, who had come to power in Germany, partly because one of his opera librettists was the Jewish writer Stefan Zweig. Strauss, by now an old man, bought a peaceful life by agreeing to work only with non-Jewish writers.

Strauss's most characteristic orchestral music is found in his tone poems, which contain a large element of programme music. The popular *Till Eulenspiegel,* based on the story of a German practical joker of the fourteenth century, is a good example. His operas range from the horrifying, tragic stories of *Elektra* and *Salome* to the light-hearted *Der Rosenkavalier,* which has echoes of his namesake JOHANN STRAUSS.

MAIN COMPOSITIONS operas: *Feuersnot* (1900), *Salome* (1905), *Elektra* (1909), *Der Rosenkavalier* (1911), *Ariadne auf Naxos* (1912), *Die Frau ohne Schatten* (1919), *Intermezzo* (1924), *Die ägyptische Helena* (1928), *Arabella* (1933), *Die schweigsame Frau* (1935), *Friedenstag* (1938), *Daphne* (1938), *Die Liebe der Danae* (1952), *Capriccio* (1942); orchestral: tone poems including *Till Eulenspiegel* (1895), *Don Quixote* (1898), *Ein Heldenleben* (1899), suites, concertos for violin, horn, oboe; 150 songs.

STRAVINSKY, IGOR FEDOROVICH (1882–1971), a Russian-born composer, startled the musical world as a young man with his bold, unconventional compositions. He adopted different styles in his later years that have not been so much admired as his early work. Stravinsky was the son of an opera singer, and was at first trained in the law. But he decided to follow a musical career, and had lessons from NIKOLAI RIMSKY-KORSAKOV. When he was twenty-six he met the great Russian ballet impresario Sergei Diaghilev, who commissioned him to write a ballet for a season in Paris. The result was *The Firebird,* and its immediate success led Stravinsky to move to Paris and then to Switzerland to write more ballets.

His third ballet, *The Rite of Spring,* with its pagan theme and apparently barbaric music, was greeted on its first performance in Paris in 1913 with a storm of boos and whistles that completely drowned the orchestra. But this only served to build up Stravinsky's fame.

The outbreak of World War I in 1914 followed by the Russian revolution of 1917 turned Stravinsky's sojourn abroad into permanent exile. He settled in France, and in time became a French citizen. In order to live he spent much of his time conducting and playing the piano, though he continued to produce a stream of compositions, including more ballets, symphonies, concertos, and operas. The death of his first wife and the outbreak of World War II in 1939 led Stravinsky to move again, this time to the United States. He settled in Hollywood, married again, and became an American citizen.

In the United States Stravinsky engaged in a series of verbal battles with leading musicologists. He also wrote a series of books about music in collaboration with the conductor Robert Craft, who acted as his musical assistant. Craft introduced him to the twelve-tone system of ARNOLD SCHÖNBERG, and many of Stravinsky's later works were written in this system. A small, fiery-tempered man, with an acid tongue and an avowed fondness for money, Stravinsky became a legend in his own lifetime.

MAIN COMPOSITIONS operas: *The Nightingale* (1914), *Mavra* (1922), *Oedipus Rex* (1927), *The Rake's Progress* (1951), *The Flood* (1962); ballets: *The Firebird* (1910), *Petrouchka* (1911), *The Rite of Spring* (1913), *The Wedding* (1923), *Apollo Musagetes* ](1928), *Persephone* (1934), *The Card Party* (1936), *Agon* (1957); orchestral: 5 symphonies, suites, concerto *Dumbarton Oaks* (1938), concertos for piano, violin; choral and vocal music: *Symphony of Psalms* (1930), *Mass* (1948), *In Memoriam Dylan Thomas* (1954), *Canticum Sacrum ad honorem Sancti Marci Nominis* (1956); chamber music; piano solos; songs. BOOKS: *Chronicles of My Life* (1935), *The Poetics of Music* (1947).

SULLIVAN, SIR ARTHUR SEYMOUR (1842–1900), an Irish-Italian organist and conductor, won lasting fame for his delightful operettas, written in conjunction with the librettist Sir William Schwenck Gilbert. He tended to despise his light music, but his serious music, on which he set much store, is now largely forgotten.

The son of an Irish clarinettist and an Italian mother, Sullivan was brought up to become, strangely enough, a typical Englishman of the day. After completing his studies, he earned his living as a teacher and organist. He became friendly with George Grove, editor of the *Dictionary of Music and Musicians*, and together the two men visited Vienna, where they rescued some of FRANZ SCHUBERT's music from oblivion. Sullivan's serious music won him among other things the friendship of members of Britain's royal family and a good social position; these enabled him to promote the cause of British musicians, who were at that time ignored by their fellow-countrymen.

Sullivan was twenty-five when he produced his first comic opera, *Cox and Box*. But it was not until he and Gilbert collaborated, first with the unsuccessful *Thespis,* and then with *Trial by Jury,* a triumph, that he got into his stride as a composer of light opera. Thanks to the impresario Richard D'Oyly Carte the two men turned out a succession of operettas that have stayed household names ever since. Their greatest success was *The Mikado,* which had an initial run of 600 performances and has been revived at frequent intervals ever since. A quarrel broke up the partnership for a time, but the two men came together again later. Sullivan's later works, particularly the serious ones, were successful in their time, but are now largely forgotten, apart from such evergreens as the hymn 'Onward Christian Soldiers' and the song 'The Lost Chord'. Sullivan's gay music is the more remarkable since he was in considerable pain from a chronic disease for much of his life.

MAIN COMPOSITIONS grand opera *Ivanhoe* (1891); operettas: *Cox and Box* (1867), *Thespis* (1871), *Trial by Jury* (1875),

*The Sorcerer* (1877), *HMS Pinafore* (1878), *The Pirates of Penzance* (1880), *Patience* (1881), *Iolanthe* (1882), *Princess Ida* (1884), *The Mikado* (1885), *Ruddigore* (1887), *The Yeomen of the Guard* (1888), *The Gondoliers* (1889), *Haddon Hall* (1892), *Utopia Limited* (1893), *The Grand Duke* (1896), *The Beauty Stone* (1898), *The Rose of Persia* (1899); oratorios: *The Prodigal Son* (1869), *The Light of the World* (1873), *The Martyr of Antioch* (1880); orchestral: symphony, overtures; songs.

TALLIS, THOMAS (*c.* 1505–85), was one of England's leading composers during the most troubled period of the Tudors. Little or nothing is known of his early life until 1542 when he became a Gentleman of the Chapel Royal, a court post. This he held during the persecutions of the Roman Catholics under Edward VI and the persecutions of the Protestants under Mary I. In 1575, during the more settled reign of Elizabeth I, Tallis and WILLIAM BYRD were jointly granted a monopoly of printing music and music paper. During his long life he wrote a great deal of Church music, including settings of the services in English, introduced as a result of the Reformation. Perhaps his greatest work is a motet in forty parts, for eight five-voice choirs.

MAIN COMPOSITIONS Church music: Latin Masses, English services, motets, anthems; secular songs; instrumental music; keyboard solos.

TARTINI GIUSEPPE (1692–1770), an Italian violinist, helped to establish the present-day style of violin playing, and wrote a number of important treatises on music. He was intended for the Church, but did not like the idea and turned to the law instead. Law too failed to please, but meanwhile Tartini had become a champion fencer, and proposed to take up the teaching of fencing as a career. A secret marriage to a fifteen-year-old niece of the Cardinal Archbishop of Padua led to his arrest, and he fled to hide in a monastery, where music was his main occupation. After some time he was found,

113

but the cardinal had by now withdrawn his opposition to Tartini's marriage. His most famous composition is the 'Devil's Trill' sonata, inspired by a dream in which the Devil played to him a sonata of surpassing beauty.

MAIN COMPOSITIONS religious works; orchestral works; chamber music; violin concertos and sonatas.

TCHAIKOVSKY, PETR ILICH (1840–93), a Russian composer, was a master of melody and orchestration. He was the son of a major-general who was also a mining engineer, and was born in a steel manufacturing town close to the Ural mountains. At the age of ten he was sent to the then Russian capital St Petersburg (now Leningrad) to school. In due course he studied law, and at the age of nineteen became a civil servant. He was already a gifted amateur musician, and at this time he began to study music seriously. When he was twenty-six he was appointed professor of harmony at the newly-opened Moscow conservatory, where he stayed for thirteen years. In the summer of 1866, Tchaikovsky had a nervous breakdown, caused by worry and overwork during the composition of his first symphony. This sort of nervous trouble recurred during the rest of his life.

Tchaikovsky took no interest at all in women, but when he was thirty-seven he suddenly married. His bride was a pupil at the conservatory, Antonina Miliukov, who had fallen in love with the composer and pursued him relentlessly. The marriage was a complete disaster, and after nine weeks Tchaikovsky fled, a nervous wreck, and tried to commit suicide. He was sent to Switzerland and Italy to recover. In the same year he had a stroke of good fortune: a wealthy widow, Nadejda von Meck, took an interest in his music and offered him an annual pension to give him freedom to compose. The two never met, though they corresponded regularly. Tchaikovsky gave up his post at the conservatory and spent his time travelling or living in the country, composing all the while. When he was forty-eight he received a further pension from the Tsar of Russia; two years later Madame von Meck stopped her allowance, possibly under pressure from her relations. Tchaikovsky's reputation as a composer and a conductor was growing steadily, but just after the first performance of his sixth and finest symphony he contracted cholera through drinking unboiled water, and died.

MAIN COMPOSITIONS operas: *The Voyevode* (1869), *Eugene Onegin* (1879), *Mazeppa* (1884), *The Little Shoes* (1887), *The Queen of Spades* (1890); ballets: *Swan Lake* (1876), *The Sleeping Beauty* (1889), *The Nutcracker* (1892); orchestral: symphonies 1–6, *Manfred* symphony, overtures, suites, concertos for piano, violin, cello; chamber music; piano solos; songs.

TELEMANN, GEORG PHILIPP (1681–1767), a German organist and musical director, was one of the most prolific composers who ever lived, and in his own day one of the most highly regarded. He founded a music society while studying law at Leipzig University, and took a post as organist at a local church. After a series of appointments at various petty courts, he settled in Hamburg as music director of the city's principal church, where he remained until his death. His facility as a composer was remarkable. GEORGE FRIDERIC HANDEL said Telemann could write a motet in eight parts as easily as anyone else could write a letter.

MAIN COMPOSITIONS 40 operas including *Pimpinone* (1725); 44 Passions; 58 Church services; 600 overtures; oratorios; cantatas; suites; concertos; chamber music.

THOMSON, VIRGIL (born 1896), an American conductor and music critic, studied in France with NADIA BOULANGER, and took back to America French ideas and innovations. He was greatly influenced by the writer Gertrude Stein. At the age of twenty-five he returned to Paris to live, and he stayed there until the Germans invaded France in 1940. He fled to the United States, and was at once offered a post as music critic of the New York *Herald Tribune*, which he kept for fourteen years. His often astringent comments earned him an international reputation. After leaving the *Herald Tribune* Thomson had a busy life as a conductor and composer, living mostly in hotels where he could indulge his passion for cooking.

His music ranges from the playfulness of his opera *Four Saints in Three Acts* (dealing with about a dozen saints in four acts), with a libretto by Gertrude Stein, to sacred works in a more sombre vein.

MAIN COMPOSITIONS operas: *Four Saints in Three Acts* (1934), *The Mother of Us All* (1947), *Lord Byron* (1968); ballet *Filling Station* (1938); orchestral: symphonies, suites, concertos, works for voice and orchestra; choral music; chamber music; piano solos; songs; incidental music; film scores. BOOKS *The State of Music* (1939), *The Musical Scene* (1945), *The Art of Judging Music* (1948), *Music Right and Left* (1951).

TIPPETT, SIR MICHAEL KEMP (born 1905), became one of the most original of English twentieth-century composers. His first job was teaching French at a school, but at the age of twenty-seven he took up adult education work in music, in which he held a succession of posts during the next nineteen years. During World War II he spent three months in jail as a conscientious objector, but his deep abhorrence of everything that Britain's Nazi enemies stood for was brought out a year or so later with his oratorio *A Child of Our Time*. As with many of his vocal works, he wrote the text himself. Tippett, unlike some of his contemporaries, used technique as a means to an end, and his use of modern idioms and harmony is balanced by a flow of melodic line that owes much to his study of Elizabethan music. He was knighted in 1966.

MAIN COMPOSITIONS operas: *The Midsummer Marriage* (1955), *King Priam* (1962), *The Knot Garden* (1970); choral: oratorio *A Child of Our Time* (1944), cantata *The Vision of St Augustine* (1966); orchestral: symphonies, suite, concerto for double string orchestra, piano concerto; chamber music; songs; song cycle *The Heart's Assurance* (1951).

116

VARÈSE, EDGARD (1883–1965), a French-born American musician, was a pioneer of the use of recorded sounds and electronic music. His early compositions were Impressionist in style, and he was largely influenced by CLAUDE DEBUSSY. At the age of twenty-four he settled in Berlin as a conductor, returning to France and military service on the outbreak of World War I. He was discharged from the army in 1915, and decided to go to America.

In New York Varèse settled down to writing a variety of what were then very strange works, such as *Ionisation,* for forty-one percussion instruments and two sirens, and *Density 21.5* for unaccompanied flute—written for a platinum flute, platinum having a density of 21.5. His ambition was to produce music that was 'just sound', free from all traditional associations, and he went to great lengths to achieve this. Many other composers have since followed in Varèse's footsteps, and the later generations of electronic compositions made entirely by tape-recorder owe much to his work. Varèse himself experimented with pure electronic music later in his career, an example being *L'Homme et la machine,* for which the composer required 400 loudspeakers.

MAIN COMPOSITIONS orchestral music; chamber music; electronic music.

VAUGHAN WILLIAMS, RALPH (1872–1958), was despite his Welsh name one of the most English of composers, and was the most important British composer of the first half of the twentieth century. Unlike so many musicians, he was slow in coming to maturity; he did not complete his formal musical education until he was twenty-nine, and a few years later he sought further lessons from MAURICE RAVEL. He began his musical career as an ardent collector of folk music, and its idiom was to influence him for the rest of his long working life. His love of English music did much to re-establish an English tradition, freed from direct influence by the music of other lands. He did a great deal to encourage music making in his own country, particularly amateur choral singing.

117

His large output covered a wide range of music—symphonies, operas, suites, concertos; it is probably his vocal music that is the most typical. He also made many arrangements of English folk music, including traditional carols.

MAIN COMPOSITIONS operas: *Hugh the Drover* (1924), *Sir John in Love* (1929), *The Poisoned Kiss* (1936), *Riders to the Sea* (1937), *The Pilgrim's Progress* (1951); ballet *Job* (1930); orchestral: 9 symphonies, suites, rhapsodies, concertos and other works for solo instrument and orchestra; choral: oratorio *Sancta Civitas* (1926), Mass, cantatas; song cycles; film scores.

VERDI, GIUSEPPE (1813–1901), was Italy's greatest composer of operas. He was the son of a tavern keeper; a wealthy friend of the family paid for his musical education. His first opera, *Oberto*, was produced in Milan when he was twenty-six. Its success earned him a contract for three more, but while he was working on the first his two small children and his wife all died. Verdi swore he would write no more operas, but was eventually tempted by a libretto based on the story of Nebuchadrezzar. The result, *Nabucco*, was a triumph, and Verdi was made.

At this time Italy was still a divided country struggling for independence. The themes of liberation that occurred in Verdi's operas made him the musical champion of a free Italy, and the demand for his operas was immense. For several years he wrote new operas at an amazing rate, the period 1851–3 including three masterpieces, *Rigoletto, La Traviata,* and *Il Trovatore*. He made a series of visits to Paris and one to London. The wealth his operas brought him enabled him to buy a country estate near Busseto. He had for some time been friendly with Giuseppina Strepponi, an opera singer, and much to the scandal of many people the couple decided to live together. They finally went through a marriage ceremony seven years later.

In 1859 and 1860 a large part of Italy was united under the rule of the King of Sardinia, Victor Emmanuel. Verdi, as one of Italy's national heroes, was persuaded to serve in the parliament of the new state, which became the kingdom of Italy in 1861. He was a senator for the next four years. By 1867 he felt perhaps he had written enough operas, but two years later he was offered a very large sum of money to write an opera to celebrate the opening of the Suez Canal. The result was *Aïda,* Verdi's masterpiece.

After *Aïda,* Verdi wrote a Requiem Mass in honour of the great Italian poet Alessandro Manzoni. He was content to rest on his laurels, but his friends conspired to persuade him to write two more operas, *Otello* and *Falstaff,* both on Shakespearean themes. After them Verdi, already over eighty years old, devoted his time to writing some sacred works. At his death he was mourned as a national hero.

MAIN COMPOSITIONS operas: *Oberto* (1839), *Un Giorno di Regno* (1840), *Nabucco* (1842), *I Lombardi* (1843), *Ernani* (1844), *Macbeth* (1847), *Luisa Miller* (1849), *Rigoletto* (1851), *Il Trovatore* (1853), *La Traviata* (1853), *Un Ballo in Maschera* (1858), *Don Carlos* (1867), *Aïda* (1871), *Otello* (1887), *Falstaff* (1893); sacred works: *Requiem Mass* (1873), *Quattro pezzi sacri* (1898); chamber music.

VICTORIA, TOMÁS LUIS (*c.* 1548–1611), one of Spain's greatest musicians, spent much of his working life in Rome. There he was ranked second only to GIOVANNI PALESTRINA, with whom he probably studied. Victoria was sent to Rome soon after being ordained a priest, King Philip II paying for his further musical education there. In Rome he became chaplain and later *maestro di cappella* to the German College, where German priests were trained. After some eleven years at the college Victoria was appointed chaplain to Philip II's younger sister Maria, widow of the Holy Roman Emperor Maximilian II. In her service he returned to Spain, but after she died in 1603 he abandoned music and spent his remaining years in quiet contemplation. In his music Victoria combined a passionate nature with sensitivity and restraint.

MAIN COMPOSITIONS *Magnificats,* hymns, motets, Masses.

119

VILLA-LOBOS, HEITOR (1887–1959), was Brazil's greatest composer. He began his musical life as a cellist, then travelled extensively around his own country collecting folktunes. When he was 35 he went to live in Paris for seven years, returning to Brazil to become director of musical education in São Paulo. Two years later he transferred to Rio de Janeiro in charge of the whole country's musical education.

Villa-Lobos produced over 2,000 compositions, in a great variety of forms and styles. He could write music anywhere and at any time. He employed several novel methods of composition, on one occasion transferring the outline of the New York skyline to graph paper, and thence to notes on the stave to provide a theme. He used the same process for a range of Brazilian mountains. His study of Brazilian folk music greatly influenced his work, and he used many of his country's traditional tunes in his compositions.

MAIN COMPOSITIONS operas: *Zoé, Malazarte*; ballets; orchestral: 12 symphonies, concertos for piano, harp, cello, guitar, harmonica, suites; chamber music including 17 string quartets; choral works; piano solos; songs.

VIOTTI, GIOVANNI BATTISTA (1755–1824), an Italian violinist, is remembered today chiefly for one work, his Concerto No. 22 in A minor. But his influence on violin playing was enormous. He was the son of a blacksmith, and a child prodigy. A rich Italian noblewoman paid for his studies, and by the time he was twenty-six Viotti was the foremost violinist in Europe. He created a sensation when he made his Paris début in 1782. Queen Marie Antoinette made him a court musician; this did not stop Viotti from walking out of a concert at Versailles when one of the French princes started talking while he was playing. Two years later Viotti left Paris suddenly and went to London, where he combined solo playing with the direction of the Italian opera there.

In 1798 he was ordered to leave London on suspicion of being a spy for France; he was allowed to return three years later, and set up a business as a wine merchant. It failed in 1818, and he managed to secure an appointment as director of the Italian opera in Paris for a few years. He died in London, heavily in debt.

Tradition has it that Viotti acted as adviser to the great bow-maker François Tourte (1747–1835). Tourte established the shape, length, and weight of the modern violin bow, and it was probably with Tourte bows that Viotti produced many of the effects that revolutionised violin playing, particularly his long, flowing runs—described by a contemporary as being 'like the flight of flaming eagles' wings'. Viotti was also one of the first soloists to use a Stradivari violin, beginning the popularity of Strads that has lasted ever since.

MAIN COMPOSITIONS orchestral: 29 violin concertos, 10 piano concertos; chamber music: string quartets, duets, sonatas.

VIVALDI, ANTONIO (1678–1741), known as *il prete rosso* (the Red Priest) from the colour of his hair, was one of the great Italian masters of the violin. He was the son of a violinist at St Mark's Cathedral, Venice, which was then one of several independent city-states that made up what is now Italy. He became a priest largely, it would seem, as a step to a secure living, but spent nearly all his time in the composition and performance of music. From the age of twenty-five until a year before he died he was associated with the Ospedale della Pietà in Venice, for much of the time as musical director. The Ospedale was a home for orphan girls specialising in music.

Vivaldi was a great programme-music man, and his most popular work, the group of violin concertos known as *The Four Seasons*, is a typical example of his love of colour and imagery. Altogether he produced around 450 concertos for a variety of instruments. As if this were not enough, he also wrote and produced forty-four operas, and a quantity of sacred music.

MAIN COMPOSITIONS concertos for violin, cello, viola

121

d'amore, trumpet, horn, oboe, flute, piccolo, bassoon, mando-
lin; 44 operas; oratorio *Judith*; cantatas; sacred works,
including motets and psalms.

WAGNER, (WILHELM) RICHARD (1813–83), a German
writer and composer, revolutionised opera. He wrote his own
libretti and supervised most details of production, in order
to ensure a completely harmonious whole. He also made
great use of what he called the *Grundthema* and later writers
have called the *Leitmotiv*—a fragment of tune connected
with a particular character, repeated whenever the character
is especially involved.

Wagner's life was turbulent. It began with a mystery. His
mother, Johanna Wagner, lost her husband, Karl Wagner,
a few months after Richard was born, and then married the
actor Ludwig Geyer, a family friend. It is at least probable
that Geyer was Richard's father. Wagner studied music from
an early age, but composition rather than an instrument.
After a short spell at Leipzig University he became chorus-
master at the theatre at Würzburg, and soon afterwards
musical director of a theatre company at Magdeburg. There
he fell in love with one of the actresses, Minna Planer, who
was four years older and had an illegitimate daughter. Two
years later he married her. Wagner's extravagant habits and
meagre pay had plunged him into debt, and in despair Minna
twice ran away from him. They were reconciled when Wagner
secured a post at Riga, in Latvia, but after two years Wagner
was again deeply in debt, lost his job, and had to leave Riga
in a hurry.

He determined to try his luck in Paris, and on his way
there met GIACOMO MEYERBEER, who gave him some useful
introductions. Wagner thanked him profusely, though he later
attacked Meyerbeer because he was Jewish. (Ironically
enough, so was Geyer.) The Wagners spent three years in
Paris in conditions of utter misery and poverty. At the end
of that time Wagner's third opera, *Rienzi*, was accepted for
performance in Dresden. Its success led to Wagner's appoint-

ment as royal *Kapellmeister* in the city. He held the post for six years; at the end of that time he became involved with some revolutionary activities, and had to flee to Switzerland, leaving as usual a load of debt behind him.

Wagner spent nearly ten years in Zurich, writing controversial books on music and drama, and making visits to other countries as a conductor. He also wrote a vast poem based on the old Scandinavian legend of the *Nibelungen*, a race of dwarfs, which he used as the libretti for four linked operas, the famous *Ring* cycle. About this time he became too intimate with the wife of a rich friend. This led to a fifteen-month separation from Minna. In 1860 he went to Paris, where a production of his opera *Tannhäuser* led to riots in the theatre. Soon afterwards he was allowed to return to Germany. Minna settled in Dresden, while Wagner wandered around trying to get his operas produced, and living with a succession of lady friends. Once again debts piled up and Wagner had to flee to Switzerland to escape his creditors.

Then came a miracle. At fifty-one, heavily in debt and not knowing which way to turn, Wagner was rescued by the eighteen-year-old King Ludwig II of Bavaria, a passionate admirer of Wagner's music. Ludwig invited him to Munich, his capital, gave him a handsome salary, and financed productions of several Wagner operas. The conductor of these operas was Hans von Bülow, with whose wife, Cosima (the illegitimate daughter of FRANZ LISZT) Wagner was having an affair. The couple had three children before Minna's death and a divorce action by von Bülow made it possible for them to marry. Because of Wagner's way of life Ludwig asked him to leave Munich, but continued to subsidise him.

By this time Wagner had completed the *Ring* cycle, and he spent several years raising money to build a special theatre at Bayreuth, in north-eastern Bavaria, where his works could be performed as he wanted. Finally, at the age of sixty-three, he saw the triumphant first performance of the *Ring* before a distinguished audience that included the emperors of Germany and Brazil.

MAIN COMPOSITIONS operas: *Die Feen* (1888), *Rienzi* (1842), *Der fliegende Holländer* (1843), *Tannhäuser* (1845), *Lohengrin* (1850), *Tristan und Isolde* (1865), *Die Meistersinger von Nürnberg* (1868); the *Ring—Das Rheingold* (1869), *Die Walküre* (1870), *Siegfried* (1876), *Götterdämmerung* (1876); *Parsifal* (1882); orchestral works. BOOKS *Art and Revolution, The Art Work of the Future, Opera and Drama, Beethoven, My Life.*

WALTON, SIR WILLIAM TURNER (born 1902), became one of the most individual English composers of the twentieth century. This may have been because, although he was a chorister at the Cathedral Choir School, Oxford, he was largely self-taught in composition. He came to the fore in the 1920s—the era of the 'bright young thing'—with *Façade*, a wickedly satirical suite for a chamber group designed to accompany a recitation of equally satirical poems by Edith Sitwell. From the music he later produced two suites for orchestra and a ballet. A few years later came his viola concerto, one of his finest works and outstanding among pieces for that instrument. It was followed by *Belshazzar's Feast*, an oratorio whose score reflects the barbaric splendour of the Babylonian court.

Later Walton wrote the music for a number of films, as well as operas, symphonies, and marches for the coronations of King George VI and Queen Elizabeth II.

MAIN COMPOSITIONS operas: *Troilus and Cressida* (1954), *The Bear* (1967); oratorio *Belshazzar's Feast* (1931); orchestral: 2 symphonies, overtures, concertos for piano, violin, viola, cello, coronation marches; film scores; chamber music; *Façade* (1923–6).

WARLOCK, PETER (1894–1930) was an English composer who is remembered equally for his music and for his work as editor, which he did under his real name of *Philip Heseltine*. His deep knowledge of music was largely self-taught, though he was helped in some measure by FREDERICK DELIUS, on whom he wrote a book. Warlock's speciality was the work of the Elizabethan madrigalists, and in his own compositions he contrived to capture much of the spirit of the Elizabethans without appearing to copy them. Warlock's music is like himself, ranging from the rollicking jollity of songs such as *Captain Stratton's Fancy* to the sadness and desolation of his song cycle *The Curlew*, settings of poems by W. B. Yeats. The melancholy side of Warlock seems to have overtaken the happy side, for it is believed that his death was due to suicide.

MAIN COMPOSITIONS orchestral: *Capriol Suite* (1927), *Serenade for Strings* (1923); choral works; chamber music; song cycles: *Lilligay* (1923), *The Curlew* (1924), *Candlelight* (1924); 100 songs; transcriptions and editions of sixteenth- and seventeenth-century music.

# WEBER, CARL MARIA FRIEDRICH ERNST VON
(1786–1826), a German conductor and pianist, liberated German opera from French and Italian influences. He became an opera conductor at the age of seventeen. After an unhappy love-affair with another man's wife, Weber married a young and charming singer, and soon afterwards secured an appointment as conductor of the German Opera at Dresden, where he stayed. In 1821 he secured a triumph with his opera *Der Freischütz* (*The Marksman*), and this brought him fame all over Europe. It was the first truly German opera, with a German theme as well as German-style music.

Weber, never strong, developed tuberculosis. His doctor advised him to go to a warm climate, but aware that he had not long to live, Weber chose instead a visit to England, where he could make a large sum of money to leave to his wife and children. He learned English especially for the visit, and so that he could write his last opera, *Oberon*, to an English libretto. *Oberon* was a great success, but a combination of the English climate and the spell of very hard work proved too much for Weber, and he died.

MAIN COMPOSITIONS operas: *Peter Schmoll* (1803), *Silvana* (1810), *Abu Hassan* (1811), *Der Freischütz* (1812), *Euryanthe*

(1823), *Oberon* (1826); incidental music for the theatre; orchestral; 2 symphonies, concertos for clarinet, piano, bassoon, overtures; cantatas; Masses; piano solos; chamber music; songs.

WEBERN, ANTON (1883–1945), was with his fellow pupil ALBAN BERG one of the most devoted followers of the twelve-tone method of composition evolved by his teacher, ARNOLD SCHÖNBERG. Webern was born in Vienna, studied there, and spent most of his life in and around the city. He held a series of conducting posts from the age of twenty-five onwards, and also taught composition. After the ending of World War II he went to Salzburg, then under American military occupation. Wandering by mistake into a forbidden area nearby, he was shot by a sentry.

Webern's music is small and delicate in texture, and small too in quantity: he wrote just thirty-one pieces. His early works, written before Schönberg had finalised the twelve-tone system, are atonal in construction—that is, they belong to no particular key. The clean, sparse texture of his writing means that every note is of importance.

MAIN COMPOSITIONS orchestral: *Passacaglia, Five Pieces for Orchestra* (1913), symphony for small orchestra, *Concerto for Nine Instruments*; chamber music; songs.

WEELKES, THOMAS (*c.* 1575–1623), was a leading English composer of madrigals. We do not know for certain, but it seems probable that he began his musical career as a chorister at Winchester Cathedral, and he was certainly organist there for about three years until 1601. He published two sets of madrigals in 1597 and 1598, and two further books, containing his finest work, in 1600. From 1601 onwards he was organist at Chichester Cathedral, though he appears to have visited London fairly regularly, and described himself as a Gentleman of the Chapel Royal. Records at Chichester show that he often got drunk and swore, but this does not seem to have stopped him playing and composing.

Weelkes was one of the contributors to *The Triumphs of Oriana* edited by THOMAS MORLEY. His madrigal was 'As Vesta Was from Latmos Hill Descending', a magnificent work in six parts that is popular to this day. He also joined Richard Deering and ORLANDO GIBBONS in bringing out a collection of settings of *The Cries of London*—150 of the tunes sung by street traders in Elizabethan times. Weelkes' work is noted for its dramatic qualities and its lively rhythms.

MAIN COMPOSITIONS Church music: 10 services, 48 anthems; 94 madrigals; chamber music; keyboard music.

WEILL, KURT (1900–50) was a German opera composer, best known for *Die Dreigroschenoper* (*The Threepenny Opera*), a topical version of *The Beggar's Opera*, written in collaboration with the poet Bertolt Brecht. This opera contains a variety of musical styles, including music-hall tunes, foxtrot, blues and a chorale, and was immensely popular. Records of one of the songs, 'Mack the Knife', sold over ten million copies.

Weill believed that there should be no distinction between 'light' and 'serious' music. His works are based on contemporary subjects, and designed to appeal to the general public through the use of popular tunes and styles. Weill had to leave Nazi Germany in 1933, and after a short period in France and England, he settled in the United States.

MAIN COMPOSITIONS operas: *The Protagonist* (1926), *Die Dreigroschenoper* (1928), *The Rise and Fall of the City of Mahagonny* (1930), *Down in the Valley* (1948); incidental music; choral works; orchestral works; film music.

WIDOR, CHARLES MARIE JEAN ALBERT (1844–1937), a French organist, is best remembered for his compositions for his own instrument, and also as a teacher of many other composers. For a very large part of his life he was professor of the organ and of composition at the Paris conservatory. Like J. S. BACH, Widor was a master of improvisation on the organ, and he was able to extend the style and scope of organ playing.

127

MAIN COMPOSITIONS orchestral; operas; ballet; chamber music; organ, including 10 *Symphonies for Organ*; piano solos, songs.

## WILBYE, JOHN (1574–1638),

was one of the greatest of English writers of madrigals, though he composed only sixty-six of them. A farmer's son, he was appointed resident musician to a wealthy land-owner, Sir Thomas Kytson, at the age of twenty-one, and spent the rest of his life in the service of the Kytson family. He specialised in serious compositions in an Italian style, sometimes setting translations of Italian texts.

MAIN COMPOSITIONS two sets of madrigals; 'The Lady Oriana' in *The Triumphs of Oriana* (1603); instrumental music; two sacred works.

## WOLF, HUGO PHILIPP JAKOB (1860–1903),

an Austrian composer, is generally regarded as second only to FRANZ SCHUBERT as a song writer. An awkward and passionate boy, he was expelled from three schools for not working at anything but his music. At the age of twenty-one he was appointed assistant conductor at the Salzburg theatre, but quarrelled with the director after only three months. Three years later he became a music critic for a fashionable paper.

In 1887 Wolf gave up his post as a critic. Given a quiet country retreat by a friend, he began to write songs at a tremendous rate, and kept up a fantastic output for four years, with only a few short breaks. Then came a three-year silence, during which time his fame steadily grew. The break ended with a Vienna concert of his music which was a great success, Brahms being among those who applauded. Inspired once more, Wolf wrote an opera, a project he had contemplated for many years. It had two performances. Wolf continued to work, supported by the generosity of his friends. But his mind was affected, and at the age of thirty-seven he was confined to a mental home.

MAIN COMPOSITIONS opera *Der Corregidor* (1895); a few orchestral pieces; *Serenade* for string quartet; about 300 songs.